CRIMINAL JUSTICE, LAW ENFORCEMENT AND CORRECTIONS

ARREST-RELATED DEATHS

STATISTICS AND COVERAGE ASSESSMENTS

CRIMINAL JUSTICE, LAW ENFORCEMENT AND CORRECTIONS

Additional books in this series can be found on Nova's website under the Series tab.

Additional e-books in this series can be found on Nova's website under the e-book tab.

CRIMINAL JUSTICE, LAW ENFORCEMENT AND CORRECTIONS

ARREST-RELATED DEATHS

STATISTICS AND COVERAGE ASSESSMENTS

MIRANDA HOUSTON
EDITOR

New York

Additional color graphics may be available in the e-book version of this book.

Library of Congress Cataloging-in-Publication Data

ISBN: 978-1-63484-992-0

Published by Nova Science Publishers, Inc. † New York

CONTENTS

Preface		**vii**
Chapter 1	Arrest-Related Deaths, 2003-2009 - Statistical Tables *Andrea M. Burch*	**1**
Chapter 2	Assessment of Coverage in the Arrest-Related Deaths Program *Duren Banks, Lance Couzens and Michael Planty*	**27**
Chapter 3	Arrest-Related Deaths Program Assessment: Technical Report *Duren Banks, Lance Couzens, Caroline Blanton and Devon Cribb*	**35**
Index		**87**

PREFACE

From 2003 through 2009, a total of 4,813 deaths were reported to the Bureau of Justice Statistics' (BJS) Arrest-Related Deaths (ARD) program. The ARD program is a national collection of persons who die in the custody or under the restraint of state or local law enforcement personnel. Deaths are reportable to the program without considering whether physical custody had been established or whether a formal arrest process had been initiated prior to the time of death. The ARD collection also includes the deaths of persons attempting to elude law enforcement during the course of apprehension. This book examines statistics and coverage assessments of arrest-related deaths.

In: Arrest-Related Deaths
Editor: Miranda Houston

ISBN: 978-1-63484-992-0

Chapter 1

ARREST-RELATED DEATHS, 2003-2009 - STATISTICAL TABLES*

Andrea M. Burch

From 2003 through 2009, a total of 4,813 deaths were reported to the Bureau of Justice Statistics' (BJS) Arrest-Related Deaths (ARD) program. Of these, about 6 in 10 deaths (2,931) were classified as homicide by law enforcement personnel, and 4 in 10 (1,882) were attributed to other manners of death. Suicide and death by intoxication each accounted for 11% of reported arrest-related deaths, accidental injury for 6%, and natural causes for 5% (figure 1). Deaths with manners classified as undetermined or those in which manners were unknown represented about 6% of reported arrest-related deaths.

During the same period, the FBI estimated nearly 98 million arrests in the United States. While men comprised about 76% of reported arrests, they represented 95% of persons who died during the process of arrest (figure 2). As a group, arrest-related decedents tended to be older than the arrest population. Those under the age of 25 accounted for 45% of reported arrests but less than a quarter (22%) of arrest-related deaths.

The ARD program is a national collection of persons who die in the custody or under the restraint of state or local law enforcement personnel.

* This is an edited, reformatted and augmented version of a report, NCJ 235385, issued by the U.S. Department of Justice, Bureau of Justice Statistics, November 2011.

Deaths are reportable to the program without considering whether physical custody had been established or whether a formal arrest process had been initiated prior to the time of death. The ARD collection also includes the deaths of persons attempting to elude law enforcement during the course of apprehension. Data collected from January 2003 through December 2009 detail the percent and type of arrest-related deaths, as well as the demographic characteristics of decedents and the law enforcement agencies involved in the death.

Arrest-related deaths are under-reported. BJS did not attempt to estimate for partial or non-responding jurisdictions. Data are more representative of the nature of arrest-related deaths than the volume at which they occur. Due to variation in reporting, caution should be used in comparing counts from year to year.

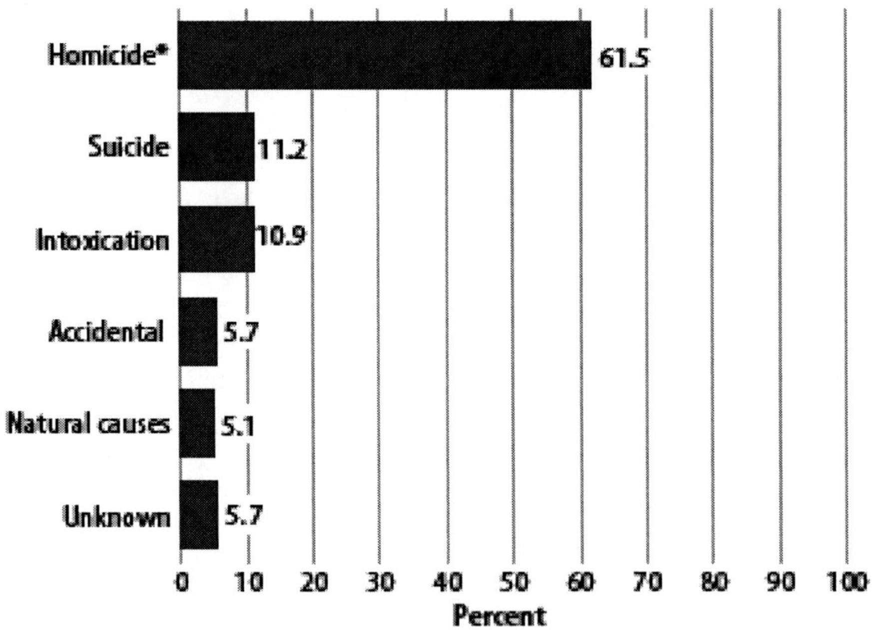

Note: Detail does not sum to total due to rounding.
*Includes homicide by law enforcement and other persons.

Figure 1. Reported arrest-related deaths, by manner of death, 2003–2009.

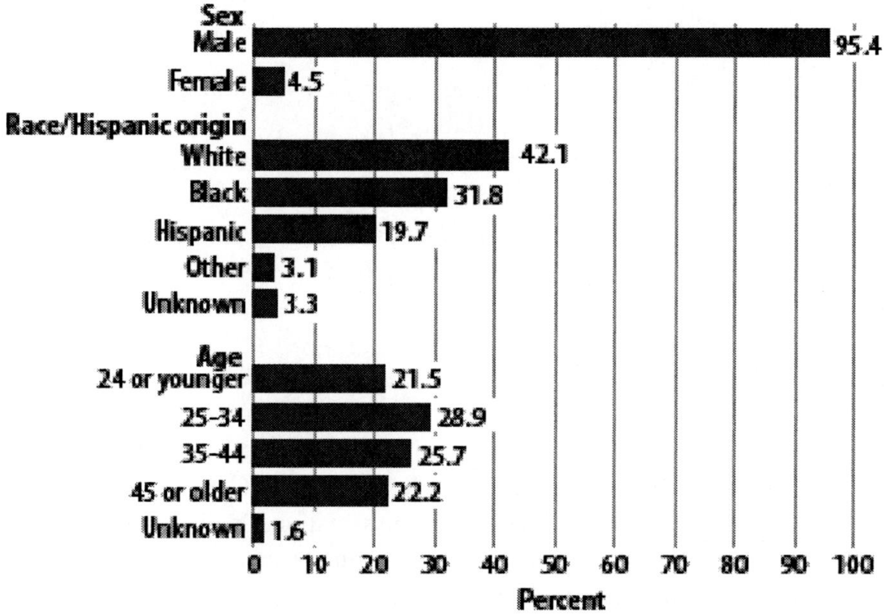

Note: Detail does not sum to total due to rounding and missing data.

Figure 2. Reported arrest-related deaths, by demographic characteristics, 2003–2009.

HIGHLIGHTS

Manner of Death

- Homicide by law enforcement personnel accounted for 2,931(61%) of reported arrest-related deaths from 2003 through 2009 (table 1).
- Suicide and death by intoxication each accounted for about 11% of reported arrest-related deaths (table 2).
- Deaths due to natural causes were the least common type of arrest-related death, comprising 5% (244) of all reported deaths.
- Of all arrest-related deaths reported from 2003 through 2009, about 6% (273) had manners of death that were either classified as undetermined or were unreported.

Decedent Characteristics

- From 2003 through 2009, males comprised 95% of all reported deaths during the process of arrest (table 4).
- Whites accounted for 42% of reported arrest-related deaths, 32% were black, and 20% were Hispanic.
- More than half (55%) of all persons who died during the process of arrest were between the ages of 25 and 44.

Manner of Death and Decedent Characteristics

- Among reported arrest-related suicides, 60% of decedents were white, 20% were Hispanic, and 15% were black (table 6).
- Of all arrest-related deaths by intoxication, blacks were 41% of reported decedents, whites were 34%, and Hispanics were 21%.
- Among males, homicide accounted for 62% of reported arrest-related deaths. Of all females, homicide represented 49% of arrest-related deaths (table 7).
- A higher percentage of female arrest-related deaths than male deaths were attributed to intoxication (16% compared to 11%) and natural causes (12% compared to 5%).
- Adults between ages 25 and 44 represented 70% of all reported arrest-related deaths due to intoxication.
- Juveniles (persons under the age of 18) comprised 3% (127) of all arrest-related deaths reported from 2003 through 2009. Most juvenile deaths (78%) were homicides.

Incident Circumstances

- The FBI estimated state and local law enforcement officers made 97.9 million arrests from 2003 through 2009. During the same period, 4,813 arrest-related deaths were reported to BJS (table 12).
- Of reported arrest-related deaths, 45% of decedents allegedly engaged in assault either immediately prior to or during the process of arrest (table 13).

- No criminal charges were intended to be filed against 163 (3%) persons who died during the process of arrest.
- Among arrest-related deaths attributed to homicide, 75% of decedents allegedly engaged in violent offenses (table 14).

Law Enforcement Agency Characteristics

- Nationwide, 7% (1,187) of state and local law enforcement agencies with 100 or more full-time sworn personnel employed 64% of these law enforcement personnel and accounted for 75% (3,613) of all reported arrest-related deaths (table 15).
- State and local law enforcement agencies employing fewer than 10 full-time sworn personnel (8,796) represented 49% of all agencies nationwide, employed 5% (34,497) of all full-time sworn personnel, and accounted for about 2% (117) of reported arrest-related deaths.

Table 1. Number of reported arrest-related deaths, by manner of death, 2003-2009

Manner of death	2003-2009	2003	2004	2005	2006	2007	2008	2009
All manners	4,813	627	673	689	721	745	629	729
Homicide — by law enforcement	2,931	376	375	377	447	455	404	497
by other persons	27	3	4	4	2	7	3	4
Suicide	541	60	84	82	67	78	76	94
Intoxication	525	83	83	90	76	89	54	50
Accidental injury	272	53	41	47	39	35	28	29
Natural causes	244	26	46	32	34	42	33	31
Unknown	273	26	40	57	56	39	31	24

Note: Due to variation in reporting, caution should be used in comparing counts from year to year. See *Methodology* for information on missing data by state for each year. Counts may differ from previous publication due to additional information.

Table 2. Percent of reported arrest-related deaths, by manner of death, 2003-2009

Manner of death	2003-2009	2003	2004	2005	2006	2007	2008	2009
All manners	100.0%	100.0%	100.0%	100.0%	100.0%	100.0%	100.0%	100.0%
Homicide — by law enforcement	60.9%	60.0%	55.7%	54.7%	62.0%	61.1%	64.2%	68.2%
by other persons	0.6	0.5	0.6	0.6	0.3	0.9	0.5	0.5
Suicide	11.2%	9.6%	12.5%	11.9%	9.3%	10.5%	12.1%	12.9%
Intoxication	10.9%	13.2%	12.3%	13.1%	10.5%	11.9%	8.6%	6.9%
Accidental injury	5.7%	8.5%	6.1%	6.8%	5.4%	4.7%	4.5%	4.0%
Natural causes	5.1%	4.1%	6.8%	4.6%	4.7%	5.6%	5.2%	4.3%
Unknown	5.7%	4.1%	5.9%	8.3%	7.8%	5.2%	4.9%	3.3%
Number of deaths	4,813	627	673	689	721	745	629	729

Note: See Methodology for information on missing data by state for each year. Percentages may differ from previous publication due to additional information.

Table 3. Number of reported arrest-related deaths, by demographic characteristics, 2003-2009

Demographic	2003-2009	2003	2004	2005	2006	2007	2008	2009
Total	4,813	627	673	689	721	745	629	729
Sex								
Male	4,594	595	645	666	688	708	600	692
Female	218	32	28	22	33	37	29	37
Unknown	1	0	0	1	0	0	0	0
Race/Hispanic origin								
White, non-Hispanic	2,026	286	274	283	302	283	258	340
Black, non-Hispanic	1,529	196	215	222	212	249	217	218
Hispanic	949	109	145	136	164	159	106	130
Other*	150	30	23	24	22	18	14	19
Unknown	159	6	16	24	21	36	34	22
Age								
17 or younger	127	18	19	13	19	20	18	20
18-24	909	118	126	141	122	146	124	132
25-34	1,391	177	186	190	239	210	182	207
35-44	1,238	184	179	190	174	192	143	176
45-54	752	94	101	83	117	119	117	121
55 or older	317	30	55	51	30	45	41	65
Unknown	79	6	7	21	20	13	4	8

*Includes American Indians, Alaska Natives, Asians, Native Hawaiians, other Pacific Islander, and persons of two or more races.

Table 4. Percent of reported arrest-related deaths, by demographic characteristics, 2003-2009

Demographic	2003-2009	2003	2004	2005	2006	2007	2008	2009
Total	100.0%	100.0%	100.0%	100.0%	100.0%	100.0%	100.0%	100.0%
Sex								
Male	95.4%	94.9	95.8%	96.7%	95.4%	95.0%	95.4%	94.9%
Female	4.5	5.1	4.2	3.2	4.6	5.0	4.6	5.1
Unknown	0.0	0.0	0.0	0.1	0.0	0.0	0.0	0.0
Race/Hispanic								
White, non-	42.1%	45.6%	40.7%	41.1%	41.9%	38.0%	41.0%	46.6%
Black, non-	31.8	31.3	31.9	32.2	29.4	33.4	34.5	29.9
Hispanic	19.7	17.4	21.5	19.7	22.7	21.3	16.9	17.8
Other*	3.1	4.8	3.4	3.5	3.1	2.4	2.2	2.6
Unknown	3.3	1.0	2.4	3.5	2.9	4.8	5.4	3.0
Age								
17 or younger	2.6%	2.9%	2.8%	1.9%	2.6%	2.7%	2.9%	2.7%
18-24	18.9	18.8	18.7	20.5	16.9	19.6	19.7	18.1
25-34	28.9	28.2	27.6	27.6	33.1	28.2	28.9	28.4
35-44	25.7	29.3	26.6	27.6	24.1	25.8	22.7	24.1
45-54	15.6	15.0	15.0	12.0	16.2	16.0	18.6	16.6
55 or older	6.6	4.8	8.2	7.4	4.2	6.0	6.5	8.9
Unknown	1.6	1.0	1.0	3.0	2.8	1.7	0.6	1.1
Number of deaths	4,813	627	673	689	721	745	629	729

*Includes American Indians, Alaska Natives, Asians, Native Hawaiians, other Pacific Islanders, and persons of two or more races.

Table 5. Number of reported arrest-related deaths, by manner of death and demographic characteristics, 2003-2009

Demographic characteristics	All manners	Homicide	Suicide	Intoxication	Accident	Natural causes	Unknown
Total	4,813	2,958	541	525	272	244	273
Sex							
Male	4,594	2,851	517	490	259	218	259
Female	218	107	24	35	13	26	13
Unknown	1	0	0	0	0	0	1
Race/Hispanic origin							
White, non-Hispanic	2,026	1,233	327	178	95	110	83
Black, non-Hispanic	1,529	937	80	217	111	85	99
Hispanic	949	599	110	109	55	29	47
Other*	150	107	12	17	4	4	6
Unknown	159	82	12	4	7	16	38

Table 5. (Continued)

Demographic characteristics	All manners	Homicide	Suicide	Intoxication	Accident	Natural causes	Unknown
Age							
17 or younger	127	99	6	5	13	0	4
18-24	909	685	80	53	54	10	27
25-34	1,391	893	140	177	65	41	75
35-44	1,238	658	159	190	78	66	87
45-54	752	390	105	84	45	75	53
55 or older	317	188	44	11	12	52	10
Unknown	79	45	7	5	5	0	17

*Includes American Indians, Alaska Natives, Asians, Native Hawaiians, other Pacific Islanders, and persons of two or more races.

Table 6. Percent of reported arrest-related deaths, by manner of death and demographic characteristics, 2003-2009

Demographic characteristics	All manners	Homicide	Suicide	Intoxication	Accident	Natural causes	Unknown
Total	100.0%	100.0%	100.0%	100.0%	100.0%	100.0%	100.0%
Sex							
Male	95.4%	96.4%	95.6%	93.3%	95.2%	89.3%	94.9%
Female	4.5	3.6	4.4	6.7	4.8	10.7	4.8
Unknown	0.1	0.0	0.0	0.0	0.0	0.0	0.4
Race/Hispanic origin							
White, non-Hispanic	42.1%	41.7%	60.4%	33.9%	34.9%	45.1%	30.4%
Black, non-Hispanic	31.8	31.7	14.8	41.3	40.8	34.8	36.3
Hispanic	19.7	20.3	20.3	20.8	20.2	11.9	17.2
Other*	3.1	3.6	2.2	3.2	1.5	1.6	2.2
Unknown	3.3	2.8	2.2	0.8	2.6	6.6	13.9
Age 17 or younger	2.6%	3.3%	1.1%	1.0%	4.8%	0.0%	1.5%
18-24	18.9	23.2	14.8	10.1	19.9	4.1	9.9
25-34	28.9	30.2	25.9	33.7	23.9	16.8	27.5
35-44	25.7	22.2	29.4	36.2	28.7	27.0	31.9
45-54	15.6	13.2	19.4	16.0	16.5	30.7	19.4
55 or older	6.6	6.4	8.1	2.1	4.4	21.3	3.7
Unknown	1.6	1.5	1.3	1.0	1.8	0.0	6.2
Number of deaths	4,813	2,958	541	525	272	244	273

*Includes American Indians, Alaska Natives, Asians, Native Hawaiians, other Pacific Islanders, and persons of two or more races.

Table 7. Percent of reported arrest-related deaths, by demographic characteristics and manner of death, 2003-2009

Demographic characteristics	Number of deaths	All manners	Homicide	Suicide	Intoxi-cation	Acci-dent	Natural causes	Un-known
Total	4,813	100%	61.5%	11.2%	10.9%	5.7%	5.1%	5.7%
Sex								
Male	4,594	100%	62.1%	11.3%	10.7%	5.6%	4.7%	5.6%
Female	218	100%	49.1	11.0	16.1	6.0	11.9	6.0
Unknown	1	100%	0.0	0.0	0.0	0.0	0.0	100
Race/Hispanic origin								
White, non-Hispanic	2,026	100%	60.9%	16.1%	8.8%	4.7%	5.4%	4.1%
Black, non-Hispanic	1,529	100%	61.3	5.2	14.2	7.3	5.6	6.5
Hispanic	949	100%	63.1	11.6	11.5	5.8	3.1	5.0
Other*	150	100%	71.3	8.0	11.3	2.7	2.7	4.0
Unknown	159	100%	51.6	7.5	2.5	4.4	10.1	23.9
Age 17 or younger	127	100%	78.0%	4.7%	3.9%	10.2%	0.0%	3.1%
18-24	909	100%	75.4	8.8	5.8	5.9	1.1	3.0
25-34	1,391	100%	64.2	10.1	12.7	4.7	2.9	5.4
35-44	1,238	100%	53.2	12.8	15.3	6.3	5.3	7.0
45-54	752	100%	51.9	14.0	11.2	6.0	10.0	7.0
55 or older	317	100%	59.3	13.9	3.5	3.8	16.4	3.2
Unknown	79	100%	57.0	8.9	6.3	6.3	0.0	21.5

*Includes American Indians, Alaska Natives, Asians, Native Hawaiians, other Pacific Islanders, and persons of two or more races.

Table 8. Number of reported arrest-related deaths, by jurisdiction, 2003-2009

Region and jurisdiction	2003-2009	2003	2004	2005	2006	2007	2008	2009
Total	4,813	627	673	689	721	745	629	729
Northeast	668	71	99	91	108	110	106	83
Connecticut	31	0	5	4	4	3	5	10
Maine	22	3	1	2	3	5	5	3
Massachusetts	42	9	6	8	2	3	10	4
New Hampshire	10	1	2	2	2	1	1	1
New Jersey	81	6	14	17	7	13	9	15
New York[a]	239	28	39	30	45	42	41	14
Pennsylvania	218	21	30	26	36	40	30	35
Rhode Island	19	2	2	1	6	3	5	0
Vermont	6	1	0	1	3	0	0	1

Table 8. (Continued)

Region and jurisdiction	2003-2009	2003	2004	2005	2006	2007	2008	2009
Midwest	822	131	124	116	101	117	105	128
Illinois	210	29	28	23	20	33	37	40
Indiana	52	9	7	10	7	7	9	3
Iowa	48	4	9	9	3	8	6	9
Kansas	41	5	6	7	9	4	4	6
Michigan	141	26	24	22	18	17	15	19
Minnesota	43	8	9	3	3	7	5	8
Missouri	26	9	3	2	2	2	3	5
Nebraska	17	5	4	1	1	3	3	/
North Dakota	7	3	2	2	0	0	0	0
Ohio	175	20	25	26	26	19	21	38
South Dakota	9	3	1	1	0	2	2	0
Wisconsin	53	10	6	10	12	15	/	/
South	1,848	217	228	252	234	309	291	317
Alabama	28	2	0	6	2	4	4	10
Arkansas[b]	6	/	0	1	3	1	/	1
Delaware	15	1	1	1	5	2	4	1
District of Columbia	20	2	4	4	2	8	/	/
Florida	523	55	68	78	76	75	81	90
Georgia[b]	8	/	/	/	/	3	2	3
Kentucky	38	3	2	4	2	6	9	12
Louisiana	54	/	1	10	12	10	7	14
Maryland[b]	19	/	/	/	/	7	9	3
Mississippi	18	/	1	0	2	5	7	3
North Carolina	143	16	19	22	/	17	34	35
Oklahoma	64	15	20	4	/	4	12	9
South Carolina	61	6	3	10	15	10	7	10
Tennessee	28	/	0	4	3	12	3	6
Texas	696	105	89	96	90	122	96	98
Virginia	113	10	17	10	22	23	11	20
West Virginia	14	2	3	2	0	0	5	2
West	1,475	208	222	230	278	209	127	201
Alaska	14	0	1	2	1	2	5	3
Arizona	238	26	46	52	57	31	8	18
California	775	106	112	93	154	118	73	119
Colorado	75	21	12	12	11	7	2	10
Hawaii	22	0	5	5	2	2	7	1
Idaho	23	2	1	1	1	8	5	5
Montana	/	/	/	/	/	/	/	/
Nevada[c]	12	2	/	/	/	/	2	8
New Mexico[c]	51	15	9	8	10	5	/	4
Oregon	77	12	13	17	12	8	8	7
Utah	69	6	9	6	9	15	8	16

Region and jurisdiction	2003-2009	2003	2004	2005	2006	2007	2008	2009
Washington	118	17	14	34	21	13	9	10
Wyoming	1	1	/	/	/	/	/	/

Note: Counts include deaths reported by states and identified by BJS staff. Due to variation in reporting practices, caution should be used in comparing jurisdictions from year to year.

/ Not reported.

[a] The New York City Police Department submits data independent of the State of New York and did not submit data in 2009.

[b] Arkansas and New Mexico cases identified by BJS staff in 2009; Georgia and Maryland cases identified by BJS staff in 2007, 2008, and 2009.

[c] In 2008, detailed data were available for 2 of the 8 records known to BJS.

Table 9. Number of reported arrest-related deaths, by jurisdiction and manner of death, 2003-2009

Region and jurisdiction	All manners	Homicide	Suicide	Intoxication	Accident	Natural causes	Unknown
Total	4,813	2,958	541	525	272	244	273
Northeast	668	387	79	92	35	58	17
Connecticut	31	21	4	1	1	3	1
Maine	22	14	4	2	1	0	1
Massachusetts	42	18	3	13	1	6	1
New Hampshire	10	7	2	1	0	0	0
New Jersey	81	47	7	9	6	8	4
New York[a]	239	118	30	38	19	28	6
Pennsylvania	218	149	27	24	5	10	3
Rhode Island	19	10	1	4	1	2	1
Vermont	6	3	1	0	1	1	0
Midwest	822	566	88	63	43	36	26
Illinois	210	142	25	18	11	11	3
Indiana	52	50	0	0	0	2	0
Iowa	48	30	12	0	4	1	1
Kansas	41	22	3	5	2	3	6
Michigan	141	94	14	15	8	7	3
Minnesota	43	33	0	4	3	1	2
Missouri	26	15	5	2	0	1	3
Nebraska	17	11	1	0	2	2	1
North Dakota	7	2	3	2	0	0	0
Ohio	175	120	15	16	10	8	6
South Dakota	9	7	2	0	0	0	0
Wisconsin	53	40	8	1	3	0	1
South	1,848	1,061	232	232	115	93	115
Alabama	28	14	5	3	0	5	1
Arkansas[b]	6	1	0	3	0	1	1

Table 9. (Continued)

Region and jurisdiction	All manners	Homicide	Suicide	Intoxication	Accident	Natural causes	Unknown
Delaware	15	13	0	1	0	0	1
District of Columbia	20	15	2	1	0	1	1
Florida	523	356	31	36	36	9	55
Georgia[b]	8	4	0	0	0	1	3
Kentucky	38	26	7	1	3	1	0
Louisiana	54	34	2	5	3	5	5
Maryland[b]	19	13	0	0	0	3	3
Mississippi	18	11	2	0	4	1	0
North Carolina	143	74	26	15	16	7	5
Oklahoma	64	51	7	3	3	0	0
South Carolina	61	34	5	10	4	2	6
Tennessee	28	17	0	5	1	2	3
Texas	696	308	127	144	40	50	27
Virginia	113	85	14	3	3	5	3
West Virginia	14	5	4	2	2	0	1
West	1,475	944	142	138	79	57	115
Alaska	14	9	4	0	1	0	0
Arizona	238	146	41	23	13	8	7
California	775	493	31	89	45	39	78
Colorado	75	41	13	6	7	3	5
Hawaii	22	8	0	4	2	4	4
Idaho	23	19	3	0	1	0	0
Montana	/	/	/	/	/	/	/
Nevada[c]	12	9	1	1	0	1	0
New Mexico[b]	51	25	17	5	2	1	1
Oregon	77	67	6	1	3	0	0
Utah	69	49	16	1	0	0	3
Washington	118	78	10	8	5	1	16
Wyoming	1	0	0	0	0	0	1

Note: Counts include deaths reported by states and deaths identified by BJS staff. Due to variation in reporting practices, caution should be used in comparing jurisdictions from year to year.

/ Not reported.

[a] The New York City Police Department submits data independent of the State of New York and did not submit data in 2009.

[b] Arkansas and New Mexico cases identified by BJS staff in 2009; Georgia and Maryland cases identified by BJS staff in 2007, 2008, and 2009.

[c] In 2008, detailed data were available for 2 of the 8 records known to BJS.

Table 10. Percent of reported arrest-related deaths, by jurisdiction and manner of death, 2003-2009

Region and jurisdiction	Number of deaths	All manners	Homicide	Suicide	Intoxication	Accident	Natural causes	Unknown
Total	4,813	100%	61.5	11.2	10.9	5.7	5.1	5.7
Northeast	668	100%	57.9	11.8	13.8	5.2	8.7	2.5
Connecticut	31	100%	67.7	12.9	3.2	3.2	9.7	3.2
Maine	22	100%	63.6	18.2	9.1	4.5	0.0	4.5
Massachusetts	42	100%	42.9	7.1	31.0	2.4	14.3	2.4
New Hampshire	10	100%	70.0	20.0	10.0	0.0	0.0	0.0
New Jersey	81	100%	58.0	8.6	11.1	7.4	9.9	4.9
New York[a]	239	100%	49.4	12.6	15.9	7.9	11.7	2.5
Pennsylvania	218	100%	68.3	12.4	11.0	2.3	4.6	1.4
Rhode Island	19	100%	52.6	5.3	21.1	5.3	10.5	5.3
Vermont	6	:	:	:	:	:	:	:
Midwest	822	100%	68.9	10.7	7.7	5.2	4.4	3.2
Illinois	210	100%	67.6	11.9	8.6	5.2	5.2	1.4
Indiana	52	100%	96.2	0.0	0.0	0.0	3.8	0.0
Iowa	48	100%	62.5	25.0	0.0	8.3	2.1	2.1
Kansas	41	100%	53.7	7.3	12.2	4.9	7.3	14.6
Michigan	141	100%	66.7	9.9	10.6	5.7	5.0	2.1
Minnesota	43	100%	76.7	0.0	9.3	7.0	2.3	4.7
Missouri	26	100%	57.7	19.2	7.7	0.0	3.8	11.5
Nebraska	17	100%	64.7	5.9	0.0	11.8	11.8	5.9
North Dakota	7	:	:	:	:	:	:	:
Ohio	175	100%	68.6	8.6	9.1	5.7	4.6	3.4
South Dakota	9	:	:	:	:	:	:	:
Wisconsin	53	100%	75.5	15.1	1.9	5.7	0.0	1.9
South	1,848	100%	57.4	12.6	12.6	6.2	5.0	6.2
Alabama	28	100%	50.0	17.9	10.7	0.0	17.9	3.6
Arkansas[b]	6	:	:	:	:	:	:	:
Delaware	15	100%	86.7	0.0	6.7	0.0	0.0	6.7
District of Columbia	20	100%	75.0	10.0	5.0	0.0	5.0	5.0
Florida	523	100%	68.1	5.9	6.9	6.9	1.7	10.5
Georgia[b]	8	:	:	:	:	:	:	:
Kentucky	38	100%	68.4	18.4	2.6	7.9	2.6	0.0
Louisiana	54	100%	63.0	3.7	9.3	5.6	9.3	9.3
Maryland[b]	19	100%	68.4	0.0	0.0	0.0	15.8	15.8
Mississippi	18	100%	61.1	11.1	0.0	22.2	5.6	0.0
North Carolina	143	100%	51.7	18.2	10.5	11.2	4.9	3.5
Oklahoma	64	100%	79.7	10.9	4.7	4.7	0.0	0.0
South Carolina	61	100%	55.7	8.2	16.4	6.6	3.3	9.8

Table 10. (Continued)

Region and jurisdiction	Number of deaths	All manners	Homicide	Suicide	Intoxication	Accident	Natural causes	Unknown
Tennessee	28	100%	60.7	0.0	17.9	3.6	7.1	10.7
Texas	696	100%	44.3	18.2	20.7	5.7	7.2	3.9
Virginia	113	100%	75.2	12.4	2.7	2.7	4.4	2.7
West Virginia	14	100%	35.7	28.6	14.3	14.3	0.0	7.1
West	1,475	100%	64.0	9.6	9.4	5.4	3.9	7.8
Alaska	14	100%	64.3	28.6	0.0	7.1	0.0	0.0
Arizona	238	100%	61.3	17.2	9.7	5.5	3.4	2.9
California	775	100%	63.6	4.0	11.5	5.8	5.0	10.1
Colorado	75	100%	54.7	17.3	8.0	9.3	4.0	6.7
Hawaii	22	100%	36.4	0.0	18.2	9.1	18.2	18.2
Idaho	23	100%	82.6	13.0	0.0	4.3	0.0	0.0
Montana	/	/	/	/	/	/	/	/
Nevada[c]	12	100%	75.0	8.3	8.3	0.0	8.3	0.0
New Mexico[b]	51	100%	49.0	33.3	9.8	3.9	2.0	2.0
Oregon	77	100%	87.0	7.8	1.3	3.9	0.0	0.0
Utah	69	100%	71.0	23.2	1.4	0.0	0.0	4.3
Washington	118	100%	66.1	8.5	6.8	4.2	0.8	13.6
Wyoming	1	:	:	:	:	:	:	:

/ Not reported.

: Not calculated for jurisdictions reporting fewer than 10 deaths during 2003-2009.

[a] The New City Police Department submits data independent of the State of New York and did not submit data 2009.

[b] Arkansas and New Mexico cases identified by BJS staff in 2009; Georgia and Maryland cases identified by BJS staff in 2007, 2008, and 2009.

[c] In 2008, detailed data were available for 2 of 8 records known to BJS.

Table 11. Number of arresting agencies with at least one reported arrest-related death, by jurisdiction, 2003-2009

Region and jurisdiction	Number of agencies in the jurisdiction*	2003	2004	2005	2006	2007	2008	2009
Total	17,985	355	372	403	388	413	361	417
Northeast	3,152	40	50	50	48	46	55	49
Connecticut	143	0	4	4	4	3	5	9
Maine	146	3	1	2	3	3	5	3
Massachusetts	357	8	5	5	2	2	10	2
New Hampshire	208	1	2	2	2	1	1	1
New Jersey	550	6	13	10	6	11	7	11
New York	514	8	11	9	10	11	8	9
Pennsylvania	1,117	11	12	16	13	13	14	13
Rhode Island	48	2	2	1	5	2	5	0
Vermont	69	1	0	1	3	0	0	1

Region and jurisdiction	Number of agencies in the jurisdiction*	2003	2004	2005	2006	2007	2008	2009
Midwest	5,572	77	80	78	68	80	61	86
Illinois	877	10	12	12	12	12	13	21
Indiana	482	8	6	6	5	6	7	2
Iowa	392	3	7	6	3	6	6	9
Kansas	371	5	4	6	7	3	3	5
Michigan	571	16	17	15	13	16	10	16
Minnesota	448	5	6	3	2	7	5	7
Missouri	576	4	3	2	2	1	3	3
Nebraska	225	4	1	1	1	1	2	/
North Dakota	114	3	2	2	0	0	0	0
Ohio	832	9	16	18	16	15	11	23
South Dakota	155	1	1	1	0	2	1	0
Wisconsin	529	9	5	6	7	11	/	/
South	7,190	131	130	158	142	172	170	188
Alabama	417	2	0	5	2	4	4	9
Arkansas	367	/	0	1	3	1	0	1
Delaware	49	1	1	1	3	2	1	1
District of Columbia	4	1	1	1	1	1	/	/
Florida	387	33	37	43	44	41	35	46
Georgia	628	/	/	/	/	3	2	3
Kentucky	388	3	1	4	2	4	6	7
Louisiana	348	/	1	8	9	8	7	13
Maryland	142	/	/	/	/	4	1	2
Mississippi	342	/	1	0	1	4	7	3
North Carolina	504	15	16	19	/	14	25	30
Oklahoma	481	12	11	3	/	2	11	5
South Carolina	272	6	3	10	13	9	7	8
Tennessee	375	/	0	3	3	7	3	6
Texas	1,913	50	42	48	47	53	46	39
Virginia	340	6	13	10	14	15	11	13
West Virginia	233	2	3	2	0	0	4	2
West	2,071	107	112	117	130	115	75	94
Alaska	50	0	1	2	1	2	3	1
Arizona	141	12	13	16	21	12	3	8
California	509	48	50	46	63	55	35	42
Colorado	246	9	9	11	8	4	1	8
Hawaii	7	0	2	2	2	1	3	1
Idaho	117	1	1	1	1	8	5	4
Montana	119	/	/	/	/	/	/	/
Nevada	76	2	/	/	/	/	2	2
New Mexico	146	7	9	7	6	4	/	3
Oregon	174	9	9	9	8	7	8	7
Utah	136	5	9	6	6	9	6	12
Washington	260	13	9	17	14	13	9	6

Table 11. (Continued)

Region and jurisdiction	Number of agencies in the jurisdiction*	2003	2004	2005	2006	2007	2008	2009
Wyoming	90	1	/	/	/	/	/	/

Note: Due to variation in reporting practices, caution should be used in comparing jurisdictions from year to year.

/ Not reported.

*Includes local police departments, sheriff offices, primary state agencies, special police agencies, and constables/marshals as reported in the 2008 Census of State and Local Law Enforcement Agencies. See appendix table 6, Census of State and Local Law Enforcement Agencies, 2008, July 2011, www.bjs.gov.

Table 12. Demographic characteristics of all reported arrests and persons who died in the process of arrest, 2003-2009

Demographic characteristics	All arrests[a]	Persons who died[b]
Total	100%	100%
Sex		
Male	75.9%	95.4%
Female	24.1	4.5
Race/Hispanic origin		
White	69.8%	42.1%
Black	27.8	31.8
Hispanicc	...	19.7
Otherd	2.4	3.1
Age		
17 or younger	15.4%	2.6%
18-24	29.2	18.9
25-34	23.8	28.9
35-44	18.0	25.7
45-54	10.3	15.6
55 or older	3.2	6.6
Offense type		
Violent	14.4%	59.8%
Property	17.4	6.4
Drug	12.6	6.4
Public order	28.2	14.5
Other	27.4	~
No charges intended	~	3.4
Unknown criminal		
behavior	~	9.5
Number of arrests and		
deaths	97,954,000	4,813

Note: Detail does not sum to total due to missing data.

... Not available.

~ Not applicable.

[a] The total number of arrests and offense type, by demographic characteristics, was estimated nationally from data reported in table 29 in Crime in the United States (2003-2009). Arrests were estimated by applying the annual percents in tables 38, 42, and 43 to the annual estimated number of arrests and summed for all years and then converted into percentages.

[b] The total number of arrest-related deaths apply to jurisdictions reporting to the program.

[c] Table 43 in the FBI's Crime in the United States presents data characterized by race, not ethnicity.

[d] Includes American Indians, Alaska Natives, Asians, Native Hawaiians, other Pacific Islanders, and persons of two or more races.

Table 13. Reported arrest-related deaths, by incident circumstances, 2003-2009

Incident circumstances	Number	Percent
All circumstances	4,813	100.0%
Violent offenses	2,878	59.8%
Homicide	233	4.8
Sexual assault[a]	49	1.0
Robbery	255	5.3
Assault	2,184	45.4
Other violent	157	3.3
Property offenses	308	6.4%
Burglary	108	2.2
Larceny	43	0.9
Motor vehicle theft	49	1.0
Other property[b]	108	2.2
Drug offenses	307	6.4%
Public-order offenses	696	14.5%
Obstruction of justice	184	3.8
Weapons	95	2.0
Traffic violations, driving while intoxicated	151	3.1
Drunkenness, disorderly conduct	154	3.2
Other public-order	112	2.3
No criminal charges intended	163	3.4%
Mental health transport	89	1.8
Medical transport	28	0.6
Unspecified	46	1.0
Offense not reported	461	9.6%

[a] Includes rape and other sexual assault.

[b] Includes arson and possession of stolen property.

Table 14. Percent of reported arrest-related deaths, by incident circumstances and manner of death, 2003-2009

Incident circumstances	All manners	Homicide	Suicide	Intoxication	Accident	Natural causes	Unknown
All circumstances	100.0%	100.0%	100.0%	100.0%	100.0%	100.0%	100.0%
Violent offenses	59.8%	75.3%	53.6%	27.2%	26.8%	25.4%	30.8%
Homicide	4.8	5.4	12.2	0.0	1.1	0.4	0.7
Sexual assault[a]	1.0	0.9	3.3	0.2	0.0	0.8	0.4
Robbery	5.3	7.0	4.8	1.5	1.5	1.6	1.8
Assault	45.4	58.2	29.2	23.6	23.2	20.1	25.3
Other violent	3.3	3.7	4.1	1.9	1.1	2.5	2.6
Property offenses	6.4%	3.3%	8.5%	11.4%	12.9%	16.0%	10.6%
Burglary	2.2	1.3	3.0	4.4	4.0	3.3	4.8
Larceny	0.9	0.4	1.7	1.7	1.1	3.3	0.4
Motor vehicle theft	1.0	0.9	1.1	0.4	3.7	1.2	0.7
Other property[b]	2.2	0.8	2.8	5.0	4.0	8.2	4.8
Drug offenses	6.4%	2.7%	4.1%	20.2%	16.2%	11.9%	9.2%
Public-order offenses	14.5%	7.9%	21.8%	24.2%	32.0%	33.6%	17.6%
Obstruction of justice	3.8	2.3	4.4	5.7	12.9	3.3	7.3
Wapons	2.0	2.4	2.6	0.8	0.4	1.6	0.4
Traffic violations, driving while intoxicated	3.1	1.1	6.3	5.1	9.9	11.5	0.7
Drunkenness, disorderly conduct	3.2	0.7	4.4	10.3	4.4	11.1	6.2
Other public-order	2.3	1.5	4.1	2.3	4.4	6.1	2.9
No criminal charges intended	3.4%	1.6%	5.0%	9.0%	1.5%	7.4%	7.3%
Mental health transport	1.8	0.7	3.1	4.4	1.5	3.7	5.1
Medical transport	0.6	0.1	1.3	2.7	0.0	0.8	0.7
Unspecified	1.0	0.7	0.6	1.9	0.0	2.9	1.5
Offense not reported	9.6%	9.2%	7.0%	8.0%	10.7%	5.7%	24.5%
Number of deaths	4,813	2,958	541	525	272	244	273

Note: Detail may not sum to totals due to rounding.

[a] Includes rape and other sexual assault.

[b] Includes arson and possession of stolen property.

Table 15. Number of law enforcement agencies, full-time sworn personnel, and reported arrest-related deaths, by agency characteristics, 2003-2009

	Law enforcement agencies		Full-time sworn personnel		Arrest-related deaths	
Characteristics of agencies	Number[a]	Percent[b]	Number[a]	Percent[b]	Number[c]	Percent
Total	17,985	100.0%	765,246	100.0%	4,813	100.0%
Type of agency involved in arrest						
Local police department	12,501	69.5%	461,063	60.3%	3,529	73.3%

	Law enforcement agencies		Full-time sworn personnel		Arrest-related deaths	
Characteristics of agencies	Number[a]	Percent[b]	Number[a]	Percent[b]	Number[c]	Percent
Sheriff's office	3,063	17.0	182,979	23.9	946	19.7
State police/highway patrol	50	0.3	60,772	7.9	273	5.7
Special jurisdiction police	1,733	9.6	56,968	7.4	44	0.9
Constables	638	3.5	3,464	0.5	10	0.2
Number of full-time sworn personnel employed by the agency involved 1–9	8,796	48.9%	34,497	4.5%	117	2.4%
10–24	4,300	23.9	67,132	8.8	248	5.2
25–49	2,402	13.4	83,349	10.9	355	7.4
50–99	1,300	7.2	89,999	11.8	458	9.5
100–249	778	4.3	115,535	15.1	694	14.4
250–499	237	1.3	83,851	11.0	610	12.7
500–999	89	0.5	60,124	7.9	466	9.7
1,000 or more	83	0.5	230,759	30.2	1,843	38.3

Note: In cases involving multiple arresting agencies, only the characteristics of the primary agency are reported.

[a] Based on the 2008 Census of State and Local Law Enforcement Agencies. Excludes agencies employing less than one full-time officer.

[b] Detail may not sum to total due to rounding.

[c] Detail does not sum to total due to missing data. Excludes 11 deaths in which type of agency was unknown and 22 deaths in which the number of full-time sworn personnel employed by the agency involved was unknown.

Table 16. Number of reported arrest-related deaths, by characteristics of the law enforcement agency involved and manner of death, 2003-2009

Characteristics of agencies	All manners	Homicide	Suicide	Intoxi-cation	Acci-dent	Natural causes	Un-known
All reported deaths	4,813	2,958	541	525	272	244	273
Type of agency involved in arrest							
Local police department	3,529	2,164	369	425	194	187	190
Sheriff's office	946	583	124	78	52	38	71
State police/highway patrol	273	174	43	17	21	8	10
Special jurisdiction police	44	28	1	3	4	7	1
Constables	10	6	0	1	1	1	1
Unknown	11	3	4	1	0	3	0
Number of full-time sworn personnel employed by the agency involved 1–9	117	57	24	14	7	10	5

Table 16. (Continued)

Characteristics of agencies	All manners	Homicide	Suicide	Intoxi-cation	Acci-dent	Natural causes	Un-known
10–24	248	134	55	27	10	12	10
25–49	355	204	61	31	21	26	12
50–99	458	253	73	53	29	18	32
100–249	694	427	64	83	38	37	45
250–499	610	399	49	64	34	26	38
500–999	466	299	43	44	32	18	30
1,000 or more	1,843	1,176	168	208	100	90	101
Unknown	22	9	4	1	1	7	0

Note: In cases involving multiple arresting agencies, only the characteristics of the primary agency are reported.

Table 17. Percent of reported arrest-related deaths, by characteristics of the law enforcement agency involved and manner of death, 2003-2009

Characteristics of agencies	All manners	Homi-cide	Suicide	Intoxi-cation	Acci-dent	Natural causes	Unknown
All reported deaths	100.0%	100.0%	100.0%	100.0%	100.0%	100.0%	100.0%
Type of agency involved							
Local police department	73.3%	73.2%	68.2%	81.0%	71.3%	76.6%	69.6%
Sheriff's office	19.7	19.7	22.9	14.9	19.1	15.6	26.0
State police/highway	5.7	5.9	7.9	3.2	7.7	3.3	3.7
Special jurisdiction	0.9	0.9	0.2	0.6	1.5	2.9	0.4
Constables	0.2	0.2	0.0	0.2	0.4	0.4	0.4
Unknown	0.2	0.1	0.7	0.2	0.0	1.2	0.0
Number of full-time sworn personnel employed by the agency	2.4%	1.9%	4.4%	2.7%	2.6%	4.1%	1.8%
10–24	5.2	4.5	10.2	5.1	3.7	4.9	3.7
25–49	7.4	6.9	11.3	5.9	7.7	10.7	4.4
50–99	9.5	8.6	13.5	10.1	10.7	7.4	11.7
100–249	14.4	14.4	11.8	15.8	14.0	15.2	16.5
250–499	12.7	13.5	9.1	12.2	12.5	10.7	13.9
500–999	9.7	10.1	7.9	8.4	11.8	7.4	11.0
1,000 or more	38.3	39.8	31.1	39.6	36.8	36.9	37.0
Unknown	0.5	0.3	0.7	0.2	0.4	2.9	0.0
Number of deaths	4,813	2,958	541	525	272	244	273

Note: In cases involving multiple arresting agencies, only the characteristics of the primary agency are reported.

METHODOLOGY

The Arrest-Related Deaths (ARD) data collection cycle begins January 1 and ends December 31 of the calendar year. State Reporting Coordinators (SRC) assist the Bureau of Justice Statistics (BJS) in collecting information regarding arrest-related deaths. The role of each SRC is to identify deaths reportable to the ARD program, compile information from valid sources regarding the circumstances related to the death, complete CJ-11 and CJ-11A data collection forms (http://www.bjs.gov), and submit data to BJS quarterly or annually. Annual data are available from 2003 through 2009 in aggregate form. All information identifying individual decedents is kept confidential.

Defining Deaths "in the Process of Arrest"

Although the *Deaths in Custody Reporting Act* of 2000 (DICRA), Public Law 106-297, mandated that all in custody deaths be counted, the legislation did not specify the meaning of the phrase "in the process of arrest." BJS staff consulted with the International Association of Chiefs of Police (IACP), the National Sheriffs' Association (NSA), and criminal justice researchers to identify which circumstances involved an arrest process. For this data collection, BJS defines "in the process of arrest" to include all circumstances in which a person is in the custody or under the restraint of law enforcement officers. This definition includes situations in which a formal arrest process was neither initiated nor intended. It includes instances in which law enforcement personnel actively pursues or attempts to apprehend a criminal suspect, regardless of whether physical custody was established. In addition, it includes deaths that involved law enforcement assistance in restraining and transporting individuals in need of medical or mental health care.

Exclusions

Deaths that occurred in a jail or other long-term holding facility and deaths that occurred in the custody of federal law enforcement officers were outside the scope of the ARD program and excluded from the analysis. All records submitted to the ARD program were cross-referenced with records submitted to BJS's Deaths in Custody Reporting Program - Jails collection in order to ensure cases were not duplicated across collections. If the death was recorded in both collections, the Jails component took priority and the record was removed from the ARD collection. The DICRA did not apply to federal law enforcement agencies. Deaths occurring in the presence of officers from federal agencies (i.e., FBI, DEA, or Marshals Service) were only reportable to the ARD program if an officer from either a state or local law enforcement agency was also present during the event causing the death. Arrest-related deaths that did not involve either a state or local law enforcement agency were excluded from the collection.

Role of State Reporting Coordinators

Participation in the ARD program is voluntary. SRCs may select any methodology—or a combination of approaches— that achieves a reliable measure of arrest-related deaths. Some methods for identifying arrest-related deaths include surveying all police departments in the state, surveying all county medical examiners or coroner's offices in the state, extracting data from other collections (i.e., FBI's Uniform Crime Reports and CDC's National Violent Death Reporting System), and conducting multi-media searches. BJS recommends SRCs do not solely rely on a system of voluntary self-reporting by state and local law enforcement agencies.

Once a reportable death is identified, the SRC is responsible for obtaining information regarding the death and completing an arrest-related death incident report (CJ-11A). Most SRCs use multiple data sources to compile information required to complete the CJ-11A incident reports. A survey of SRCs conducted in 2007 indicated that of the 47 states participating in the ARD program at some point between 2003 and 2006, 42 used multiple sources to obtain information on arrest-related deaths, while 30 states reported at least 3 different sources of data.

State and local law enforcement agencies were the most common source of data used by SRCs. Law enforcement agencies voluntarily reported arrest-related deaths to 40 data providers. In California and Texas, law enforcement agencies were required by state law to submit arrest-related deaths. The SRCs were asked to work with the law enforcement agency involved in the death to collect the information requested on the CJ-11A form. In instances where the law enforcement agency involved in the death did not complete the CJ-11A form, the SRC was asked to obtain information from official source documents (such as a police report or death certificate) or indirectly through oral communication, press releases from the involved law enforcement agency or medical office, legal proceedings, or other vetted sources of information. Media accounts of the event and death were not considered sources of official information.

Appendix Table 1. Agencies reporting arrest-related death records, 2006

Agencies	Number of agencies
All data providers	48
State criminal justice commission	22
State attorney general	8
State police/highway patrol	8
State department of correction	5
State medical examiner	3
State department of public safety	1
State office of financial management	1

Subsequently, SRCs were discouraged from using media accounts of the event as their primary source of information when completing the CJ-11A form. In the event that the SRC could not obtain information from any other source, BJS authorized the use of media accounts to supplement incomplete CJ-11A forms.

Program Coverage

The ARD program was initiated in order to comply with requirements set forth in the DICRA. The legislation required the U.S Department of Justice to begin a quarterly collection of individual death records for all persons incarcerated in local jails, state prisons, juvenile correctional facilities, as well as "any person who is in the process of arrest." Since the expiration of the DICRA legislation in 2006, BJS has continued to collect ARD data, but no longer requires quarterly submissions.

As the statistical agency for the Justice Department, BJS began implementing the ARD data collection in 2003. When the DICRA was enacted, only California and Texas (each pursuant to state law) conducted a statewide count of all arrest-related deaths. In the remaining 48 states and the District of Columbia, the ARD program was the first attempt to perform a comprehensive count of all deaths occurring during the process of arrest. The attorneys general of California and Texas agreed to complete statewide reports of arrest-related deaths for submission to BJS. In all other jurisdictions, BJS worked with state officials to determine which agency would collect arrest-related death reports.

During reporting year 2006, a state criminal justice commission, commonly administered by the governor's office was the most common data reporting contact (22 states), followed by the state attorney general and state police department (8 states each) (see appendix table 1). In five states, the department of corrections took a lead role in compiling records. In over 30 states, the reporting office also served as a state criminal justice Statistical Analysis Center (SAC).

While every state identified a data provider, three states— Georgia, Maryland, and Montana—did not submit records during the 2003-2009 collection periods. Forty-seven states and the District of Columbia participated in the collection at some point, but the participation of some states varied by year. (See appendix table 2 for a summary of state reporting participation.) Although a jurisdiction may not have participated in the ARD program in a given year, arrest-related deaths may have been identified and reported by BJS staff.

In an effort to increase the ARD program's national coverage, BJS began exploring the use of internet-based searches to retrospectively identify arrest-related deaths occurring from 2007 through 2009. BJS staff conducted online media searches based on 12 key terms and identified websites dedicated to either in-custody deaths or deaths associated with the usage of specific weapons, such as conductive energy devices. Once an arrest-related death was identified, all available information was sent to the appropriate SRC for verification and follow-up. The SRC was asked to complete a CJ-11A form using official source documents and then return the form to BJS.

More detailed information is available at www.bjs.gov.

Appendix Table 2. States not reporting arrest-related deaths in all years, 2003–2009

Region and jurisdiction	2003	2004	2005	2006	2007	2008	2009
Arkansas	/	□	□	□	□	/	/
District of Columbia	□	□	□	□	□	/	/
Georgia	/	/	/	/	/	/	/
Louisiana	/	□	□	□	□	□	□
Maryland	/	/	/	/	/	/	/
Mississippi	/	□	□	□	□	□	□

Region and jurisdiction	2003	2004	2005	2006	2007	2008	2009
Montana	/	/	/	/	/	/	/
Nebraska	□	□	□	□	□	□	/
Nevada	□	/	/	/	/	□	□
New Mexico	□	□	□	□	□	/	/
New York*	□	□	□	□	□	□	□
North Carolina	□	□	□	/	□	□	□
Oklahoma	□	□	□	/	□	□	□
Tennessee	/	□	□	□	□	□	□
Wisconsin	□	□	□	□	□	/	/
Wyoming	□	/	/	/	/	/	/

□ Reported.

/ Not reported.

* The New York City Police Department did not submit data to the State of New York in 2009.

In: Arrest-Related Deaths
Editor: Miranda Houston
ISBN: 978-1-63484-992-0

Chapter 2

ASSESSMENT OF COVERAGE IN THE ARREST-RELATED DEATHS PROGRAM*

Duren Banks, Lance Couzens and Michael Planty

EXECUTIVE SUMMARY

After the passage of the Death in Custody Reporting Act (DICRA) of 2000 (P.L. 106-297), the Bureau of Justice Statistics (BJS) began collecting data on deaths that occurred in the process of arrest. Provisions in the 2000 DICRA called for collecting all deaths occurring within the process of arrest in any state, county, or local law enforcement agency nationwide. From 2003 through 2009, BJS obtained reports on 4,813 such deaths through its Arrest-Related Deaths (ARD) program. About 3 in 5 of these deaths (2,931) were classified as homicides by law enforcement personnel. The remaining 2 in 5 deaths were attributed to other manners, including suicide (11%), intoxication deaths (11%), accidental injury (6%), and natural causes (5%).[1] In three-quarters (75%) of homicides by law enforcement personnel, the underlying offense of arrest was a violent offense. No criminal charges were intended in less than 2% of these incidents.

To assess the completeness of the ARD data that BJS received, in 2013 BJS undertook a technical review of the ARD program's methodology and an assessment of the program's coverage of all arrest-related deaths in the United

---

* This is an edited, reformatted and augmented version of a technical report, NCJ 249099, issued by the U.S. Department of Justice, Bureau of Justice Statistics, October 2015.

States. The methodology review examined the variation in states' approaches to identifying and confirming arrest-related deaths. The assessment of coverage focused on determining whether BJS received all arrest-related deaths that occurred or only a portion of them. The primary focus of the assessment of coverage was on homicides by law enforcement officers.

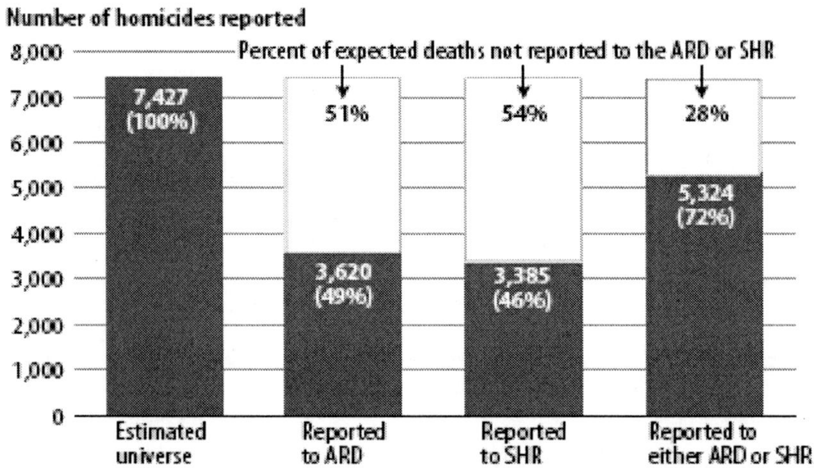

Source: Bureau of Justice Statistics, Arrest-Related Deaths (ARD) program, 2003–2009 and 2011; and FBI, Supplementary Homicide Reports (SHR), 2003–2009 and 2011.

Figure1. Estimated number of law enforcement homicides and percent not reported, by data source, 2003–2009 and 2011.

The analysis showed that the ARD program obtained fewer law enforcement homicide deaths than expected, based on the methodology used to estimate the expected number of law enforcement homicides. It also showed that the data BJS used for comparison purposes—the FBI's Supplementary Homicide Reports (SHR)—also reported fewer justifiable homicides than expected.[2] In total, the BJS ARD program data and the SHR data each identified about half of the expected number of homicides by law enforcement officers during the period from 2003 through 2009 and 2011 (figure 1). The ARD program captured approximately 49% of these homicides, while the SHR captured 46%. More than a quarter (28%) of law enforcement homicides in the United States were not captured by either system. The analysis also showed that the ARD program obtained more arrest-related deaths in 2009 and 2011, when BJS began to use open source methods (e.g., Google searches to identify potential cases), compared with prior years when BJS did not use open source methods.[3]

Drawing from the results of this study, BJS has begun a pilot study that explores multiple methods of identifying and confirming deaths occurring in the process of arrest. The study will inform BJS efforts to implement the requirements of the reauthorized 2013 DICRA (P.L. 113-242).

ARREST-RELATED DEATHS PROGRAM ASSESSMENT

BJS designed the ARD program to be a census of all deaths that occurred in the process of arrest or during an attempt to obtain custody by a state or local law enforcement agency. BJS collected ARD data from 2003 through 2013, covering deaths occurring in calendar years 2003 through 2012.[4] BJS implemented the ARD program as part of its Deaths in Custody Reporting Program (DCRP), which it developed in response to the 2000 DICRA and includes collections that measure deaths occurring in jails and state prisons, in addition to deaths occurring during the process of arrest.[5, 6]

The ARD program identified the manner of arrest-related death, including law enforcement homicides, other homicides, accidents, suicides, and deaths due to natural causes. Law enforcement homicides included all deaths attributed to weapons or restraint tactics used by state or local law enforcement officers. From 2003 through 2009, about 61% of all deaths reported to the ARD program were law enforcement homicides.[7]

As part of its ongoing efforts to evaluate the quality of its statistical programs, BJS began to assess the quality of ARD program data in 2013. This assessment focused on the methodology used to obtain the data and on the completeness of the arrest-related deaths reported to the program. In part, BJS began this assessment in response to an unexpected increase in the number of law enforcement homicides reported to the ARD program in 2009 and 2011. In these years, BJS began to use open sources (e.g., web searches and Google Alerts) and other methods to independently identify potential cases of deaths in the process of arrest. These cases were then sent to BJS's state data collection agents for review and verification. The implementation of this new methodology led to an increase in the number of homicides by law enforcement reported to the ARD that was more than the average number (406) for previous years. For example, BJS obtained 689 reports of law enforcement homicides in 2011, which represented a 39% increase from the 496 reported in 2009 (figure 2).

Given the increase in the number of deaths identified by the ARD program after changes in methodology, along with concerns about overall program coverage, BJS temporarily suspended ARD data collection while it undertook the ARD program assessment and technical review. A primary focus of this BJS study was to estimate the coverage error (i.e., the percentage of the expected number of ARD deaths that the program missed).

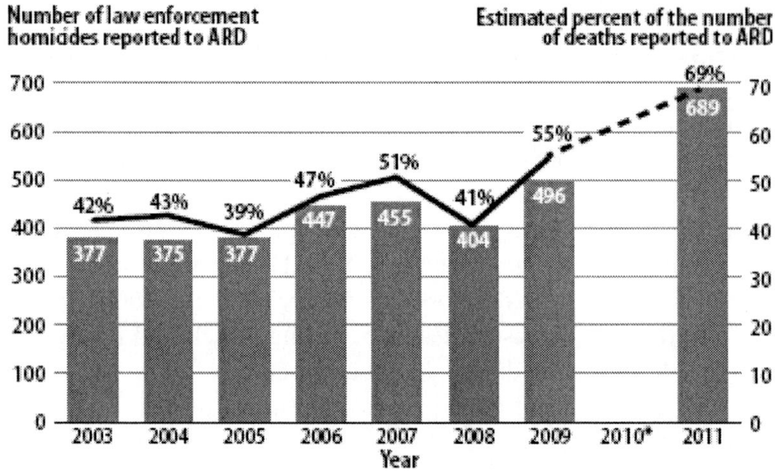

Source: Bureau of Justice Statistics, Arrest-Related Deaths (ARD) program, 2003–2009 and 2011.

*2010 data not released.

Figure 2. Number of law enforcement homicides reported to the ARD program and estimated, lower bound, 2003–2009 and 2011.

Methodology Review and Coverage Assessment

The ARD program had methodological limitations that prevented BJS from obtaining a full enumeration of all arrest-related deaths in the United States. The program relied on voluntary reporting from state and local agencies to compile information about arrest-related deaths, including law enforcement homicides. It also relied on centralized reporting mechanisms to compile and submit information about these deaths. These state reporting coordinators (SRC) in each of the 50 states and the District of Columbia were responsible for understanding the scope and definition of the ARD program, identifying eligible cases in their respective states, and working with available resources to collect and report information about those cases. Not all states had an SRC. In those states, BJS relied on its contractor to take on the SRC role. As of 2009, several jurisdictions (i.e., Arkansas, the District of Columbia, Georgia, Maryland, Montana, Nevada, Wisconsin, and Wyoming) had yet to participate in the program.

BJS studied the completeness of all law enforcement homicides reported to the ARD program by using both ARD data and a separate source of data on law enforcement homicides—the FBI's SHR data.[8] BJS compared the number of law enforcement homicides reported by the ARD program from 2003 through 2009 and 2011, representing all of the ARD program years for which data were available, with the number of justifiable homicides captured by the SHR over the same period.[9]

Applying a commonly used technique known as capture-recapture to estimate the size of populations, the BJS assessment produced an estimate of the expected number of law enforcement homicides in the United States. This estimate was based on the extent to which the ARD and SHR data on law enforcement homicides overlapped (i.e., reported on the same cases).[10] As the amount of overlap between the data sources increased, the estimated underlying population size got closer to the number of cases in the data sources.

Capture-recapture analysis relies on a number of assumptions, including that cases can be matched across lists, that the lists are limited to cases that meet the definition of law enforcement homicides, and that inclusion on one list is independent from inclusion on the other. Many of these assumptions were met, but the nature of the ARD program and SHR necessitated the violation of other assumptions (including independence across lists, as some ARD SRCs relied on the same reporting mechanisms as those that inform the SHR). RTI International implemented a number of adjustments to account for these violations.[11]

In the assessment, BJS generated estimates based on differing assumptions about missing data. This resulted in an upper- and a lower-bound estimate of the expected number of law enforcement homicides that should have been reported to the ARD program, if the ARD data were 100% complete.

Across the 8 years of data used in the analysis from 2003 through 2009 and 2011, the lower-bound estimate of the expected number of law enforcement homicides that should have been reported to the ARD program was 7,427, or an average of 928 per year (table 1). The ARD program captured approximately half (49%) or 3,620 of these homicides (an average of 453 a year), whereas the SHR captured 46% or 3,385 of these homicides (423 per year). More than a quarter (28%) or 2,103 of the estimated homicides in the United States during those 8 years were not captured by either system. The lower-bound estimate assumed that any agencies that did not report to the ARD or SHR programs did not have an arrest-related death during the study period. The upper-bound estimate assumed the number of arrest-related deaths in law enforcement agencies that did not report to the ARD or the SHR were comparable to those of the agencies that did report. This yielded an estimated 9,937 law enforcement homicides in the United States, an average of 1,242 per year, of which the ARD program captured more than a third (36%).

Table 1. Number and percent of law enforcement homicides captured, by source and estimation approach, 2003–2009 and 2011

	Lower-bound estimate		Upper-bound estimate	
Law enforcement homicides	Number	Percent of universe	Number	Percent of universe
Estimated universe	7,427	100%	9,937	100%
Observed deaths	5,324	72%	5,324	54%
ARD	3,620	49	3,620	36
SHR	3,385	46	3,385	34
Unobserved deaths	2,103	28%	4,613	46%

Source: Bureau of Justice Statistics, Arrest-Related Deaths (ARD) program, 2003–2009 and 2011; and FBI, Supplementary Homicide Reports (SHR), 2003–2009 and 2011.

As BJS implemented changes to improve the ARD collection methodology, the program's coverage of arrest-related deaths improved. Analysis indicated that the ARD program included a greater proportion of the estimated law enforcement homicides in 2009 and 2011 than it did from 2003 through 2008. In 2011, the ARD program captured 69% of the estimated 1,000 law enforcement homicides in the United States (figure 3).

CONCLUSION

BJS's analysis of the ARD program's coverage found that for the study period from 2003 through 2009 and 2011, both the ARD program and the SHR obtained reports for only about half of the expected number of law enforcement homicides in the United States. Examining the data on deaths that were reported to either or both systems, BJS found that, combined, the systems obtained reports on at best 72% of all law enforcement homicides in the United States across all years observed. The ARD program showed improvements in coverage in the most recent years studied (i.e., 2009 and 2011), and these improvements coincided with the increased use of open-source data to identify potential cases of arrest-related deaths. Despite demonstrated improvements over time, the ARD program missed reports for more than a quarter of the expected number of law enforcement homicides in 2011.

The ARD program coverage may be improved by providing a more centralized method for identifying arrest-related deaths and providing incentives for law enforcement agencies to confirm or identify deaths that occur during the process of arrest and to provide information about them. Therefore, BJS has begun to explore the use of open-source data to identify arrest-related deaths in conjunction with a direct survey of law enforcement and other agencies responsible for investigating deaths in the process of arrest. The study will inform BJS efforts to implement the requirements of the reauthorized DICRA of 2013 (P.L. 113-242).

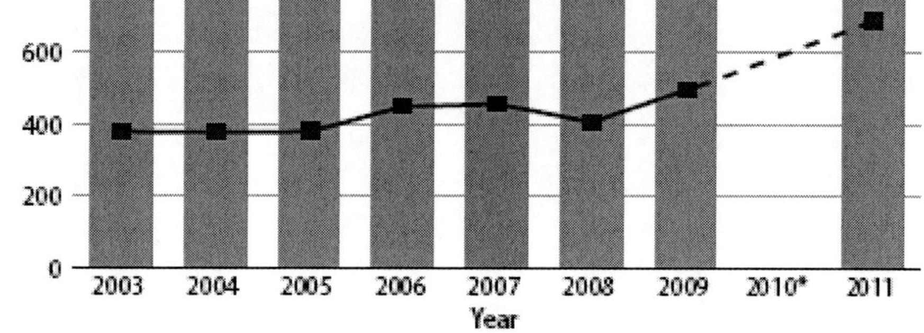

Source: Bureau of Justice Statistics, Arrest-Related Deaths (ARD) program, 2003–2009 and 2011.

*2010 data not released.

Figure 3. Number of law enforcement homicides reported to the ARD program and estimated, unadjusted coverage, 2003–2009 and 2011.

End Notes

[1] Arrest-Related Deaths, 2003–2009 - Statistical Tables (NCJ 235385, BJS web, November 2011).

[2] Arrest-related Deaths Program Assessment: Technical Report (NCJ 248543, BJS web, March 2015).

[3] ARD program data for 2010 were unavailable due to a shift in data collection methodology between 2009 and 2011.

[4] BJS only published statistics from calendar years 2003 through 2009.

[5] The 2000 DICRA expired in 2006, although BJS continued to maintain its DCRP data collections. The 2013 DICRA was passed by Congress and became law in December 2014. The 2013 DICRA requires any state receiving funds from the Department of Justice to report on a quarterly basis information regarding the death of any person who is detained, under arrest, or in the process of being arrested; is en route to be incarcerated; or is incarcerated.

[6] For more information on the Deaths in Custody Reporting Program, see the BJS website.

[7] See Arrest-Related Deaths, 2003–2009 - Statistical Tables (NCJ 235385, BJS web, November 2011).

[8] SHR data are voluntarily provided by law enforcement agencies to the FBI's Uniform Crime Reports (UCR) Program. For more information about the UCR program, see https://www.fbi.gov/about-us/cjis/ucr/ucr.

[9] The UCR Program handbook defines justifiable homicides as (1) the killing of a felon by a police officer in the line of duty or (2) the killing of a felon, during the commission of a felony, by a private citizen.

[10] See Palusci, V.J., Wirtz, S.J. & Convington, T.M. (2010). Using capture-recapture methods to better ascertain the incidence of fatal child maltreatment. Child Abuse & Neglect, 24, 396–402. See also Wolter, K.M. (1986). Some coverage error models for census data. Journal of the American Statistical Association, 81, 338–346.

[11] For descriptions of the violations, see Arrest-Related Deaths Program Assessment: Technical Report (NCJ 248543, BJS web, March 2015).

In: Arrest-Related Deaths
Editor: Miranda Houston

ISBN: 978-1-63484-992-0

Chapter 3

ARREST-RELATED DEATHS PROGRAM ASSESSMENT: TECHNICAL REPORT*

Duren Banks, Lance Couzens, Caroline Blanton and Devon Cribb

EXECUTIVE SUMMARY

The Bureau of Justice Statistics (BJS) designed the Arrest-Related Deaths (ARD) program to be a census of all deaths that occur during the process of arrest in the United States. The manner in which these data were collected varied from state to state, and often depended on the data systems available to the state reporting coordinators (SRCs) responsible for data collection throughout the state, the involvement of local law enforcement agencies or medical examiner's/coroner's offices, and other support that the SRC may have had to conduct the data collection. This variability in approach has led to questions about whether these data collection methods were capable of capturing the universe of arrest-related deaths and law enforcement homicides in particular. BJS requested RTI International to conduct an assessment of the ARD program to evaluate (1) the coverage of the program in comparison to Supplementary Homicide Reports (SHRs) maintained by the Federal Bureau of Investigation (FBI) and (2) various aspects of the current program

* This is an edited, reformatted and augmented version of a contracted report, NCJ 248543, issued by the U.S. Department of Justice, Bureau of Justice Statistics, March 2015.

methodology. The coverage assessment matched law enforcement homicides captured by the ARD program to those found in the SHR justifiable homicide file, followed by a capture-recapture analysis to provide information on the scope and characteristics of cases eligible for inclusion in the ARD program that are captured in one or both of these data systems. The ARD law enforcement homicides and SHR justifiable homicide files are similar; however, some law enforcement homicides that were not classified as justifiable are not identified in the SHR.

RTI calculated the size of the law enforcement homicide population in the United States and the ARD program coverage using two methods to estimate the lower and upper bounds of ARD coverage. We found that over the study period from 2003 through 2009 and 2011, the ARD program captured, at best, 49% of all law enforcement homicides in the United States. The lower bound of ARD program coverage was estimated to be 36%. These findings indicate that the current ARD program methodology does not allow a census of all law enforcement homicides in the United States.

The ARD program captured approximately 49% of law enforcement homicides, while the SHR captured 46%. An estimated 28% of the law enforcement homicides in the United States are not captured by either system. However, the methodology for identifying ARD cases has changed over the observation period. In 2011, the ARD program was estimated to cover between 59% and 69% of all law enforcement homicides in the United States, depending on the estimation method used. While this coverage estimate still does not result in a census, it does suggest improvements over time in the overall approach to identifying law enforcement homicides and reporting them to the ARD program.

We found considerable variability between states in the proportion of law enforcement homicides that are reported to the ARD program only, the SHR only, or to both sources in 2011. Twelve states reported only to the ARD program in 2011, while no states reported cases only to the SHR. Additional analyses to explore the effect of case identification methodology and SRC affiliation failed to identify a specific ARD methodology that was associated with better program coverage in 2011.

The current analyses only compared ARD program coverage to the SHR. Other sources may also provide additional information about the extent of law enforcement homicides in the United States or in selected jurisdictions, and coverage of the various data collection systems. These sources include the Fatal Injury Reports that are part of the National Vital Statistical System maintained by the Centers for Disease Control and Prevention and direct reports from local law enforcement agencies. In addition, the ARD program assessment examined only arrested-related deaths that are the result of law enforcement homicides. Arrest-related deaths due to illness, overdose, accidents, and other manners of death are likely even more difficult to identify and, if included, could have a significant downward impact on our coverage estimates. However, no other national data collection exists that examines arrest-related deaths due to a manner other than law enforcement homicide. If BJS pursues a collection to measure law enforcement homicides or all manners of arrest-related deaths in the United States, changes must be made to the data collection methodology to support more complete coverage.

1. BACKGROUND

By definition, the Arrest-Related Deaths (ARD) program was to be a national census of law enforcement homicides that occurred during the process of arrest or during an attempt to obtain custody by a state or local law enforcement agency in the United States. The program was implemented by the Bureau of Justice Statistics (BJS) in 2003 as part of its Deaths in Custody Reporting Program (DCRP) in response to the Deaths in Custody Reporting Act of 2000 (DICRA). In addition to the ARD program, the DCRP includes collections that measure deaths occurring in jails and state prisons.

The ARD program methodology relied on state reporting coordinators (SRCs) in each of the 50 states and the District of Columbia. SRCs were responsible for understanding the scope and definition of the ARD program, identifying eligible cases in their state, and working within available resources to collect and report information about those cases. The manner in which these data were collected varied from state to state, and often depended on the data systems available to the SRC, the involvement of local law enforcement agencies or medical examiner's/coroner's offices, and other support that the SRC may have had to conduct the data collection. This variability in approach led to questions about whether the existing data collection methods were capable of capturing the universe of arrest-related deaths and law enforcement homicides in particular.

The Supplementary Homicide Reports (SHRs) represent another national-level data source that provides information on law enforcement justifiable homicides in the United States.[1] The SHR is part of the Uniform Crime Reporting (UCR) Program conducted by the Federal Bureau of Investigation (FBI). While the UCR summary program provides aggregate annual counts of the number of homicides occurring in the United States, the SHR data provide additional details about each homicide incident, including the jurisdiction, month, year, victim and offender demographic characteristics, weapon, the circumstances surrounding the incident (e.g., argument, robbery, gang-related), and the relationship between the victim and offender, if known.

To determine whether the ARD program met the criteria for a valid and reliable statistical collection, BJS tasked RTI to undertake a program assessment to better understand the utility of the ARD data collection approach and to effectively assess alternative approaches. RTI conducted the ARD program assessment to evaluate (1) the homicide coverage of the program in comparison to the Supplementary Homicide Reports (SHRs) and (2) the current program methodology. The coverage assessment matched ARD cases to the SHR. A capture-recapture analysis provided information on the scope and characteristics of cases eligible for inclusion in the ARD program that are captured in one or more of these data systems. The program methodology assessment further compared ARD cases identified by various approaches currently employed by the state reporting coordinators (SRCs) and the ARD staff, including media searches, access to state reporting systems, and direct reporting from law enforcement agencies. The program assessment process and findings are documented below.

2. Methodology

The Arrest-Related Deaths (ARD) program relied on a census collection from agencies that experienced one or more deaths to estimate the number of arrest-related deaths in a particular calendar year. Because the census was (1) obtained through self-reporting by agencies, as opposed to targeted collection of a probability sample derived from a robust agency frame, and (2) included no agencies that did not experience a death, it is difficult to make inferences regarding any undercoverage using information from the ARD program alone. In light of these constraints, a coverage assessment that utilizes comparable data from an auxiliary source is appropriate.

The U.S. Department of Justice, through the Federal Bureau of Investigation (FBI), releases annual law enforcement-reported homicide data in the form of Supplementary Homicide Reports (SHRs). Because the SHR data provide incident-level information on homicides, they can be used to help assess the coverage of the ARD data collection. Whereas the ARD collection documents all manners of death that occur during the arrest process or in the presence of law enforcement, the SHR is limited to homicides and therefore does not include suicide, accidents, illness or natural causes, drug intoxications, and other manners of death not considered to be homicides. Therefore, to make comparisons between these data collections, each must be restricted to a similar population of cases. For the analyses presented below, we restricted the SHR to only the subset of homicides in which an offender is killed by the police (justifiable homicides) and subset the ARD to those incidents defined as homicides committed by law enforcement. Both of these subsets are limited to incidents involving state or local law enforcement agencies. The SHR and ARD data sets include all law enforcement homicides reported in the years that the ARD program produced annual datasets: 2003 through 2009 and 2011. Some states did not report any SHR data in some years. With the exception of Florida, which did not report any SHR data for the entire period, no additional information was added to the FBI's SHR file for other states. Homicide cases for Florida were collected independently from the FBI collection and added to the SHR file for this analysis.

By linking ARD decedent records to those captured in the SHR, it is possible to make inferences about the total size of the law-enforcement homicide population and, thereby, about the population coverage achieved in the ARD program. This analytic technique, known as capture-recapture, is typified by studies of wild animal populations, though it is widely used in the study of human populations as well, particularly in coverage evaluation for censuses (Wolter, 1986). Though the ARD coverage assessment is based on traditional capture-recapture methods, unique characteristics of ARD data necessitate special techniques, including probabilistic record linkage between data sources and adjustments for unobserved agencies.

2.1. Probabilistic Case-Level Linking

Capture-recapture analysis depends on the ability to link records across data sources. In wildlife applications, this requirement is easily met as captured animals are identified through tagging. In the context of a coverage assessment utilizing an auxiliary data source not collected as part of the coverage study, this requirement becomes more difficult. Because decedents are not uniquely identified across data sources (by name or Social Security number, for example), record linkage must be based on comparable decedent demographic and incident characteristics in an attempt to create a unique link. However, linkages made without unique identifiers are inherently uncertain, decedents are matched between ARD and SHR sources probabilistically based on measured similarity between records, within a monte carlo replication framework. This means that although a given ARD decedent will be linked to either no SHR decedents or a single SHR decedent in a particular replicate, the nature of the link for that ARD decedent (whether it is linked and, if so, to which SHR decedent) is allowed to vary across replicates according to the probabilities associated with particular record pairings, based on measured similarity between cases. Probabilistic linking is random in nature and incorporates additional uncertainty into the process of estimating population coverage; monte carlo replication allows for this additional uncertainty to be captured in variance estimates.

2.1.1. Calculation of Similarity Scores

Records cannot be uniquely identified across sources so linking decedent records is done probabilistically, based on the measured similarity between two records. The first step in determining link probabilities for a given ARD decedent and the decedent's potential matches in the SHR is to calculate a similarity score. Similarity is based on the following variables that are common to both ARD and SHR:

- Originating Agency Identifier (ORI)
- Sex
- Year
- Date reported/date of death
- Age
- Race/Hispanic origin

Decedent records are considered 0% similar if they do not match on at least ORI, sex, and year and are not eligible for linking. For records that have common values for these three variables across sources, scores are calculated based on the values of the date, age, and race/Hispanic origin variables. These measures include a mix of continuous and categorical variables; therefore, the method for calculating the similarity score must account for both types.

The portion of the similarity score determined by the continuous variables (date and age) is calculated as a function of the standard Euclidean distance for two variables, such that two records having identical values across sources have a similarity of 1. The portion of the similarity score determined by the continuous variables approaches 0 as dates and ages become more dissimilar.

The portion of the similarity score determined by the race/Hispanic origin values is based on a penalized scoring approach described in Boriah et al. (2008). This approach assigns a similarity of 0 if the variables disagree across sources and a value of less than 1 when the variables agree. The amount that matching records' similarity score is discounted is determined by the probability that the race/Hispanic origin value would be in agreement by random chance alone. This approach is based on the premise that matches that have a high probability of occurring by random chance should not count as much as those that would be observed very rarely by chance alone. The final similarity score is calculated as a weighted mean of the components based on continuous variables (weight = 2/3) and race/Hispanic origin (weight = 1/3).

Once similarity scores are calculated for each potential pairing of a given ARD decedent and SHR decedents from the same ORI, sex, and year, these values are used to create an additional score. This score represents the combined dissimilarity between the ARD case and all of its potential matches. Following calculation of this dissimilarity score, all scores are scaled such that their sum is 1. These scaled scores are treated as relative probabilities and determine how cases are linked. A detailed description of similarity score calculation, including all formulas, may be found in appendix A.

2.1.2. Thresholds for Matching

Potential record pairings fall into one of two categories: those that are within a predetermined threshold of similarity and those that are not. If two records each have the same value of ORI, sex, year, and race/Hispanic origin, there is a difference in the dates of report and death less than or equal to 30 days, and there is a difference in recorded age of less than or equal to 5 years[2], the pairing is thought to be within an acceptable threshold to consider the records as representing the same decedent. In these instances, the scaled similarity scores (match probabilities) for all pairings for the same ARD decedent that are not within threshold are set to 0. This includes the scaled dissimilarity score, which represents the joint probability across potential pairings that no SHR record represents the same decedent. This means that when an ARD decedent has one or more pairings that are within threshold, the probability that the record will not be linked at all is 0. In some cases, a single ARD case may have more than one pairing that is within threshold. In these instances, a link will take place according to probabilities resulting from rescaling the similarity scores among only the within-threshold pairings such that they sum to 1. ARD decedent records that have a single potential pairing that is within threshold undergo the same rescaling process, resulting in a single potential pairing with a link probability of 1; these pairings are thereby referred to as certainty pairings. For ARD decedent records with no potential within-threshold pairings, linking occurs according to the probabilities associated with all potential pairings and the calculated probability that no pairing is correct. Thus, these decedent records may remain unlinked, and in the event that all potential pairings are very dissimilar, this will be the most probable outcome.

2.1.3. Linking Algorithm

The first step in the linking process is separating ARD and SHR decedent records into two groups: those that have ORI, sex, and year values common across data sources and those that do not. The latter group is considered unlinkable; those records with common values of ORI, sex, and year are linked probabilistically according to the following steps (a more technical description is provided in appendix B):

1) **Randomly sort the ARD cases within ORI, sex, and year.** The first step in linking ARD decedent records to the SHR is a random sort. Because the ARD decedents are processed sequentially and a linked SHR decedent is unavailable for linking to other ARD records processed after the link is made, it is important to ensure that that the order in which the ARD cases are processed is not fixed. This is necessary for monte carlo replication as described in 2.1.4.
2) **For each ARD case, calculate a similarity score corresponding to each SHR case with the same ORI, sex, and year.** In this step, similarity scores are calculated as described in 2.1.1, above. Note that for any ARD decedent record that is not the first to be processed in its ORI, sex, and year classification, there may be SHR decedents ineligible for linking, as they are linked to other ARD records processed previously. The similarity scores for such ineligible pairs are set to 0.
3) **Treating the scores from (2) above as probabilities, calculate the dissimilarity score (the probability that the ARD case is not represented by any SHR decedent in the same ORI, sex, and year).** Given the small number of variables that overlap between the ARD and SHR and the inability to perfectly match across sources, it is important to assign a nonzero probability to the possibility that the ARD decedent is not represented by any of the SHR decedent records in the same ORI, sex, and year.

4) **Determine the number of cases that are within threshold.** Each potential pairing for a given ARD decedent is checked against the threshold criteria described in 2.1.2. If one or more pairings are within threshold, all other scores (including the one described in (3), above) are set to 0.
5) **Scale scores.** Though the scores described above may be individually interpreted as probabilities, their sum may be greater than 1, complicating both their joint interpretation and the process of linking. In this step, each of the scores is divided by their sum, maintaining their relative proportions. Note that as a result of (2) and (4) above, several outcomes are possible:
   i. No potential SHR decedent records have been previously linked to other ARD records, and there are no within-threshold potential pairings—in this case there will be a nonzero probability that no linkage will be made.
   ii. No potential SHR decedent records have been previously linked to other ARD records and there is one potential within-threshold pairing—in this case the within-threshold pairing is a certainty.
   iii. No potential SHR decedent records have been previously linked to other ARD records and there are multiple potential within-threshold pairings—in this case, a linkage will be made only according to the probabilities among within-threshold pairings, as all other probabilities have been set to 0 prior to scaling.
   iv. One or more potential SHR decedent records have been previously linked to other ARD records and there are one or more potential SHR records available for linking —these cases are then treated identically to i. through iii., above.
   v. One or more potential SHR decedent records have been previously linked to other ARD records and there are no potential SHR records remaining for linking—in this case, the probability that the ARD decedent record is not represented in the SHR is 1 and the record is not linked.

2.1.4. Monte Carlo Replication

The inability to precisely match decedents between the ARD and the SHR necessitates a probabilistic linking approach, but this technique is inherently random in nature, achieving the most probable outcomes only in expectation. By repeating the linking algorithm many times, the variability resulting from that randomness can be incorporated into final estimates.

The monte carlo framework leverages two points at which randomness enters the linking process: the use of random numbers for sorting ARD decedent records and the use of random numbers to select from potential pairings. This means that uncertainty in record linking resulting from the lack of overlapping variables, and/or errors in variables that do overlap, will be incorporated in final estimates.

Generation of random number streams depends on selecting 'seed' values—numbers that are fed into the algorithm as a starting point for generating the stream. By setting random number seeds in a predictable way (for repeating the results) that is a function of both the replicate number and the ORI, sex, and year grouping, variation inherent to the probabilistic linking can be correctly accounted for. Given the resource-intensive nature of probabilistic linking in general, a replicate count of 1,000 was selected to balance resource usage and precision.

2.2. Capture-Recapture Analytic Approach

Once decedent records have been linked across the ARD and SHR, capture-recapture methods can be used to estimate the total population of law enforcement homicide and, thereby, the proportion of that population covered by the ARD program. This analysis makes use of the commonly applied Lincoln-Petersen (LP) estimator, with modifications for bias amelioration necessitated by the characteristics of the ARD program.

Use of the basic LP estimator implies acceptance of several assumptions, including the following:

a) The population of interest is closed geographically and in time and is of fixed size;
b) Correct matches may be made between sources;
c) Each data source is free of spurious cases, such as those that are out of scope or that are duplicates;
d) The probability of inclusion is independent across lists;
e) The probability of inclusion is constant within lists; and
f) The probability of inclusion is constant across lists.

For the purposes of evaluating ARD coverage, some of the above assumptions may be accepted as true, while others must be accepted with qualification and, in some cases, in conjunction with specific analytic techniques designed to minimize the biases incurred as a result of their likely violation. Given the goal of the analysis—to determine if ARD coverage is high enough to justify continuing the program in its current form—violation of some assumptions is not as problematic as would be the case in other applications because the direction of incurred bias is known. This allows for reasonable assertions of upper limits for ARD coverage, which provides sufficient information given the circumstances.

In addition to the assumptions presented as a.–f. listed above, this analysis must account for an additional, and seemingly unique, challenge: estimating the impact that unobserved law enforcement agencies with law enforcement homicides have on decedent population coverage. Because agencies with law enforcement homicides report inconsistently to the ARD and SHR, proper evaluation of coverage must account for whether or not agencies that are not observed in either source experienced law enforcement homicides, and, if so, how many. Sections 2.2.1 and 2.2.2, below, address two methods of conducting the capture-recapture analysis, including assumptions made and the benefits of each technique. A detailed, technical description of the techniques employed is provided in appendix B.

2.2.1. Simple Poststratified Lincoln-Petersen Approach

This approach is the simpler of the two described here, as it does not incorporate any correction for unobserved agencies. In other words, under this approach there is an implied assumption that any agency not observed in either the ARD or the SHR has not experienced a law enforcement homicide, or, put another way, this method assumes that every agency with homicides is observed in at least one source. Though this assumption is strong (and very likely violated), the results of this method are still quite useful given the context in which they're being used. Specifically, assuming that all unobserved agencies are so-called 'true zeroes' (they have not experienced any cases of law enforcement homicide), results in a coverage estimate that represents the best-case scenario. Thus, the simple, poststratified LP estimate may be interpreted as an upper bound for ARD coverage, with the true coverage rate falling somewhere below. From a decision-making perspective, knowing the best-case estimate may be sufficient, especially if the estimated coverage is considered unacceptable.

2.2.1.1. Assumptions

Assumptions a. and c. from 2.2 are accepted as valid in this approach. With both sources limited to cases from 2003–09 and 2011, and all arising from U.S. agencies, assumption a. is reasonable. Because each source has been subset to the common subpopulation of justifiable law enforcement homicides, and BJS has verified that no duplicates are included in the files provided, assumption c. is also reasonable.[3]

As stated previously, given the inability to uniquely identify decedents across data sources, assumption b. cannot be reasonably made. Conducting the analyses within a monte carlo replication framework allows for incorporation into final estimates of error incurred through violation of this assumption, and for this reason, no single replicate can be evaluated for linking correctness. Individual linkages may be made in a single replicate with low probability, though across replicates they will occur rarely. Taken as a whole, across all replicates, average linking outcomes represent the best matches given the available agency and individual information.

Assumption d., commonly referenced in the context of behavioral response in capture-recapture literature, cannot be validated and potential biases incurred through violation cannot be mitigated or quantified given the information available. It is worth noting, however, that the nature of this bias may not be particularly important for this analysis. In the context of this study, a behavioral response would mean that those responsible for collecting and reporting data to the ARD and SHR programs would be more or less likely to report to one program if they had already reported to the other. Because (1) it is reasonable to assume that such an effect could work in both directions (i.e., a record may be more or less likely to be captured in one source if it has been previously captured in the other) and (2) there is no reason to believe that one source consistently captures decedent records before the other, any bias resulting from behavioral responses is assumed to be diffused and to contribute little, if any, directional bias to final coverage estimates.

Homogeneity of capture probabilities implied by assumptions e. and f. cannot be guaranteed within or across data sources, so the LP estimator of population size may contain downward bias, leading to an overestimation of coverage (Wolter, 1986). The common method for dealing with this bias—and the one employed in this analysis—is poststratification. Once decedent records are linked, they are grouped into strata corresponding to the cross-classification of available demographic characteristics. The simple LP estimator is then used within strata and the results are aggregated over the complete population. This approach is based on the idea that, once grouped, capture probabilities become homogeneous within strata. Poststratification on these variables may not account for all bias because the number of reliable characteristics with enough samples per category common to both sources is low (race/Hispanic origin and age only). Again, in the context of this analysis, remaining bias may have little to no effect on the analytic utility of the results, as the direction of the bias (if not its magnitude) is known. Heterogeneity in capture probabilities yield population size estimates that are deflated and coverage rates that are artificially high. Thus, final coverage estimates can be interpreted as the upper bounds on the actual coverage rate.

2.2.1.2. Strengths and Limitations

This simple LP estimator method has the notable benefit of being the simpler of the two methods implemented, as it does not require estimation of the number of unobserved agencies with law enforcement homicides. Additionally, this method yields an estimate that represents the best-case scenario for ARD coverage. From the perspective of a user wanting to know the most accurate coverage estimate, rather than its upper boundary, this method is not ideal.

2.2.2. Poststratified Lincoln-Petersen Approach with Constant Ratio Adjustment for Unobserved Agencies

Unlike the approach described in 2.2.1, the poststratified LP method rejects the assumption that any agency not observed in either the ARD or the SHR has not experienced a law enforcement homicide. It therefore must account for two additional unknown factors: the number of unobserved agencies with law enforcement homicides and the number of homicides experienced among those agencies.

Under this approach, the simple LP estimator is used to estimate the total number of agencies that experienced law enforcement homicides in the reference period. By treating the ratio of this estimate over the number of agencies actually observed across both sources as an agency undercoverage adjustment factor, decedent population estimates corresponding to each poststratum (as described in 2.2.1) may be extrapolated to represent the decedent population among unobserved agencies. Because the decedent population is inflated by a constant factor, this approach implies a strong assumption that missing agencies with homicides are missing at random (i.e., the distribution of missing agencies in terms of decedent counts is identical to that of the observed agencies).[4] Notably, agencies that are captured in both the ARD and SHR have, on average, more homicides than those observed in only one source (5.2 vs. 1.5), and it may be reasonable to infer that unobserved agencies are more like the latter group. In other words, assuming that missing agencies are just like those that have been observed likely results in an inflationary bias in the decedent population size estimate and, therefore, a deflationary bias in the corresponding ARD coverage estimate. This implies that the coverage estimate derived using a constant ratio adjustment for unobserved agencies represents a worst-case scenario, or lower bound, for ARD coverage. Presenting the coverage estimates derived using this method along with the one described in 2.2.1 yields a bounded range representing the most extreme assumptions regarding the nature of unobserved agencies. Given the requirements of the analysis, this is likely sufficient and benefits from making as few assumptions as possible.

2.2.2.1. Assumptions

Beyond the assumptions inherent to the agency undercoverage adjustment factor noted above, the assumptions for this model are identical to those described in 2.2.1.1 and are not repeated here.

2.2.2.2. Strengths and Limitations

The postratified LP methodology provides additional benefit over that described in 2.2.1 in that it rejects the (likely false) assumption that all unobserved agencies are so-called true zeroes. The notable downsides of this approach are the necessity of making additional assumptions regarding the nature of unobserved agencies—each additional assumption introduces new sources of potential error. Additionally, as this method treats unobserved agencies as being like those that are observed, in terms of the volume of law enforcement homicides, it potentially yields a deflated coverage estimate.

2.2.3. Data Assumptions and Coverage Estimate Implications

The sections discussed above deal with theoretical assumptions underpinning the LP estimator. As noted, these assumptions have been addressed where possible and, in all cases, their potential effects on coverage estimates have been discussed. Given the context in which these estimates are being used and the careful statements regarding their interpretation, the analysis is robust to violations of these assumptions. Fundamental assumptions about the data, however, are largely unverifiable.

For certain data items, specifically date and race/Hispanic origin variables that are used in linking and that are measured differently across sources, comparability is maximized through recoding (as noted in appendixes A and C) and the impact of remaining inconsistencies can be inferred based on the amount of variability in final estimates across replicates, as the linking procedure results in cases being linked probabilistically even when dates and race/Hispanic origin codings are not in agreement across data sources. Because the range of final ARD coverage estimates across replicates is less than 2 percentage points, it is reasonable to infer that inconsistencies in these variables across sources do not have a large impact. Furthermore, the small range of replicate estimates indicates that final estimates are not being driven by the probabilistic linking.

Across replicates, 68% of decedent records remain unmatched after linking. Of these unmatched records, 53% come from ARD and an overwhelming 82% of those are not even eligible to enter the probabilistic linking procedure because they have no match in the SHR on ORI, year, and sex. Given the relative rarity of female law enforcement homicides and the low estimated probability of decedent records appearing in the incorrect year, ORI can be viewed as the linking variable with by far the largest impact on final estimates. Data quality issues relating to ORI codes may therefore affect estimated coverage estimates, though, unfortunately, errors resulting from problems with ORI codes are of an unknown magnitude and direction.

3. FINDINGS

3.1. Arrest-Related Death Coverage

As requested by BJS, RTI estimated the size of the law enforcement homicide population in the United States and the Arrest-Related Death (ARD) program coverage using two methods. The simple, poststratified Lincoln-Petersen method assumes that all nonreporting law enforcement agencies did not have any law enforcement homicides during the observation period. This approach provides the highest possible ARD coverage estimate and the lowest estimate of the total population size (also referred to as the “right bookend” approach). Following this approach, the ARD coverage of all law enforcement homicides is estimated to be 48.73%, with a 95% confidence interval ranging from 47.28% to 50.18%. In other words, the ARD program captured about half of all law enforcement homicides in the United States during the observation period.

The second coverage estimate assumes that all nonreporting agencies have the same number of law enforcement homicides as agencies that did report to either the Supplementary Homicide Reports (SHRs) or the ARD program. The poststratified Lincoln-Petersen approach with a constant ratio adjustment for unobserved agencies provides the “left bookend” or lower estimate of ARD coverage. Under this approach, the ARD program is estimated to capture 36.43% of all law enforcement homicides in the United States, with a 95% confidence interval ranging from 34.50% to 38.35%.

Figure 1 is a Venn diagram of the ARD and SHR coverage following the simple, poststratified Lincoln-Petersen method (the first coverage estimate described above), which assumes that all nonreporting law enforcement agencies did not have any law enforcement homicides during the observation period. Under these assumptions, the universe of law enforcement homicides in the United States across all years examined (2003–09 and 2011) is 7,427, or an average of 928 law enforcement homicides per year. The ARD program captures approximately 49% of these homicides, while the SHR captures 46%. About 28% of the law enforcement homicides in the United States are not captured by either system (see figure 2).

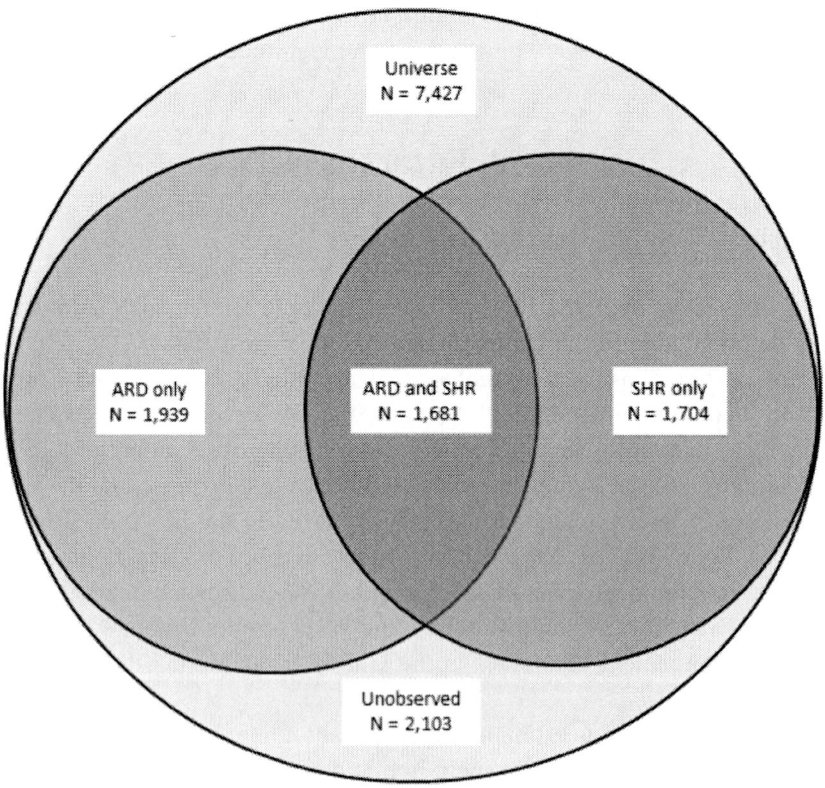

Figure 1. ARD and SHR coverage and overlap of the universe of law enforcement homicides in the United States, with no agency adjustment, 2003–09 and 2011.

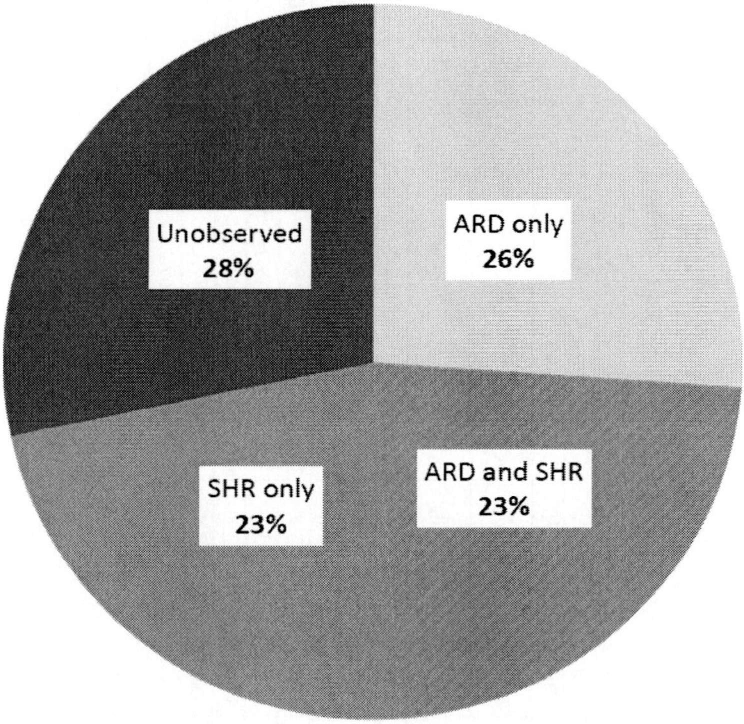

Figure 2. Estimated proportion of law enforcement homicide universe covered by each source, with no agency adjustment, 2003–09 and 2011.

RTI implemented a monte carlo replication approach to match SHR and ARD cases (see table 1). There were an estimated 5,324 law enforcement homicides reported to either system in the observed years. More than two-thirds of those homicides were not able to be matched across data sources. The level of unmatched cases was greatest in 2005 (75.6%) and lowest in 2011 (60.4%). Certainty matches across sources are created when cases match on the originating agency identifier (ORI) number, year, and sex, within 1 month of date of death (or date of report for SHR) and within 5 years for age. Across all observed years, approximately 21% of all law enforcement homicides reported to either source were certainty matches, ranging from 15% in 2008 to 26% in 2009 and 2011. These certainty matches represent 94.5% of ARD cases with one or more SHR pairings satisfying the certainty criteria noted above (not shown). The remaining 5.5% have more than one match that satisfies the certainty criteria (4.9% have two matches, and the remaining 0.6% have between three and six matches).

Table 1. ARD and SHR law enforcement homicides, by match outcome, 2003–09 and 2011

			Probability match score								Certainty match		Total	
ARD program data collection year	No match		0.01 – 0.25		0.26 – 0.50		0.51 – 0.75		0.76 – 0.99					
	AVG N	%	AVG N	%	AVG N	%	AVG N	%	AVG N	%	AVG N	%	AVG N	%
All LE homicides	3,643.9	68.4	221.0	4.2	190.1	3.6	150.8	2.8	6.8	0.1	1,111.9	20.9	5,324.5	100
2003	424.6	71.3	23.6	4.0	19.3	3.2	15.2	2.5	0.1	0.0	112.6	18.9	595.3	100
2004	416.7	70.6	18.9	3.2	19.4	3.3	11.8	2.0	0.6	0.1	123.1	20.8	590.4	100
2005	456.7	75.6	19.8	3.3	16.8	2.8	14.8	2.5	1.8	0.3	94.4	15.6	604.3	100
2006	469.8	70.9	22.7	3.4	27.0	4.1	24.4	3.7	0.1	0.0	118.4	17.9	662.4	100
2007	450.1	66.2	25.2	3.7	23.2	3.4	21.1	3.1	1.5	0.2	158.9	23.4	680.0	100
2008	482.6	73.4	37.1	5.6	21.1	3.2	18.5	2.8	0.0	0.0	98.0	14.9	657.3	100
2009	443.4	62.7	30.1	4.3	27.7	3.9	17.2	2.4	1.2	0.2	187.1	26.5	706.7	100
2011	500.1	60.4	43.6	5.3	35.7	4.3	27.8	3.4	1.5	0.2	219.4	26.5	828.0	100

Note: The 'AVG N' represents the mean count across all replicates.

Table 2. ARD law enforcement homicides, by match outcome, 2003–09 and 2011

			Probability match score											
	No match		0.01 – 0.25		0.26 – 0.50		0.51 – 0.75		0.76 – 0.99		Certainty match		Total	
ARD program data collection year	AVG N	%	AVG N	%	AVG N	%	AVG N	%	AVG N	%	AVG N	%	AVG N	%
All LE homicides	1,939.5	53.6	221.0	6.1	190.1	5.3	150.8	4.2	6.8	0.2	1,111.9	30.7	3,620.0	100
2003	206.3	54.7	23.6	6.3	19.3	5.1	15.2	4.0	0.1	0.0	112.6	29.9	377.0	100
2004	201.4	53.7	18.9	5.0	19.4	5.2	11.8	3.1	0.6	0.2	123.1	32.8	375.0	100
2005	229.3	60.8	19.8	5.3	16.8	4.5	14.8	3.9	1.8	0.5	94.4	25.0	377.0	100
2006	254.4	56.9	22.7	5.1	27.0	6.0	24.4	5.5	0.1	0.0	118.4	26.5	447.0	100
2007	225.0	49.5	25.2	5.5	23.2	5.1	21.1	4.6	1.5	0.3	158.9	34.9	455.0	100
2008	229.3	56.8	37.1	9.2	21.1	5.2	18.5	4.6	0.0	0.0	98.0	24.3	404.0	100
2009	232.7	46.9	30.1	6.1	27.7	5.6	17.2	3.5	1.2	0.2	187.1	37.7	496.0	100
2011	361.0	52.4	43.6	6.3	35.7	5.2	27.8	4.0	1.5	0.2	219.4	31.8	689.0	100

Note: The 'AVG N' represents the mean count across all replicates.

There were 3,620 cases reported to ARD in the years observed (see table 2). Across all years, 54% of those were not able to be matched to an SHR case, and 31% were a certainty match. Probability matches included 11.4% of ARD cases with a low probable match (probability score of 0.50 or less), and 4.4% with a probability match score between 0.51 and 0.99. Among all matched ARD cases, 47.6% were linked to a single SHR case across replicates (not shown), and 74.7% were matched to five or fewer distinct SHR cases. The maximum number of distinct SHR pairings for a single ARD case across replicates was 24. Across years, the lowest overlap with the SHR occurred in 2005 when 61% of all ARD cases were not able to be matched to an SHR case. In 2009, however, 38% of ARD cases were a certainty match to SHR, 15% were a probable match, and 47% were a no match. Figure 3 further shows the distribution of match scores for cases reported to ARD across all years observed.

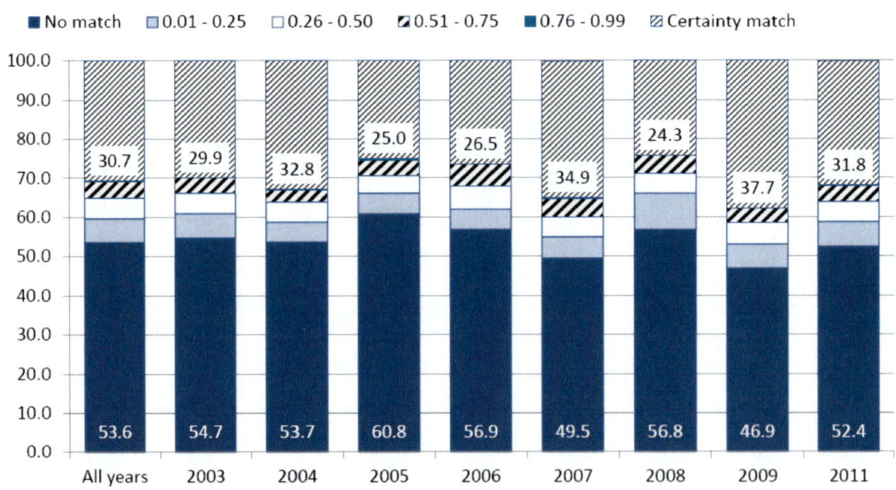

Figure 3. Percent of observed ARD law enforcement homicides, by match score, 2003–09 and 2011.

Table 3 describes characteristics of law enforcement homicides reported to either the SHR or the ARD program by match score. As expected, law enforcement homicide victims with an unknown age are more likely to have no match. Law enforcement homicide victims that are identified as white, non-Hispanic (75%) are most likely to have a no match compared to other race/Hispanic origin groups, while victims of an "other" race are most likely to have a certainty match (26%) compared to unknown or other unspecified race/Hispanic origin groups.

The characteristics of cases reported to the ARD program by probability match score are described in table 4. Cases with victims of any unknown age are more likely to have no match compared to any known age group. Similarly, cases with victims of an unknown race/Hispanic origin are more likely to have a low probability match score compared to any known race/Hispanic origin groups. ARD cases with a victim identified as Hispanic (28%) are least likely to result in a certainty match compared to other known race/Hispanic origin groups.

As described in appendix C, the race/Hispanic origin variable is measured differently by each data source, and there is a high amount of missing data regarding Hispanic origin in the SHR. This measurement issue may account for some of the differences in probability match scores by race/Hispanic origin group. A subgroup analysis on states with larger proportions of Hispanic populations was conducted to provide further insight into whether the difference in probability match scores across race/Hispanic origin groups is meaningful. RTI calculated coverage estimates among five states that report Hispanic origin to SHR greater than 75% (Arizona, California, North Carolina, Pennsylvania, and Texas). Following the simple, poststratified Lincoln-Peterson approach (upper bound), the ARD coverage in these five states is 71.91% (95% confidence interval range from 69.47% to 74.34%). With agency adjustment (providing the lower bound), the estimated ARD coverage is 54.90% in these five states (95% confidence interval range from 50.52% to 59.29%). Given the wide range of these results, it is likely that they are confounded with other, unmeasured agency characteristics, such as agency size, reporting requirements, and the prevalence of law enforcement homicides. That is, the estimates with these five states were intended to act as sensitivity analyses for measuring the Hispanic origin of victims of arrest-related homicides; however, they suggest that other variables may be driving ARD program coverage estimates.

Table 5 describes the characteristics of law enforcement homicides that were reported to the ARD program, the SHR, or both. No differences emerged in cases reported to either system or to both in terms of age and race/Hispanic origin of the victim. The vast majority of all law enforcement homicides resulted from a firearm, with no difference in the proportion of homicides resulting from other means (e.g., other weapon) across data sources. Across ARD program years, there does not appear to be a difference in the characteristics of cases captured by the ARD Program, the SHR, or both.

Table 3. ARD and SHR law enforcement homicides, by matching variable and match outcome, 2003–09 and 2011

Matching variable	No match		Probability match score								Certainty match		Total	
			0.01 – 0.25		0.26 – 0.50		0.51 – 0.75		0.76 – 0.99					
	AVG N	%	AVG N	%	AVG N	%	AVG N	%	AVG N	%	AVG N	%	AVG N	%
All LE homicides	3,643.9	68.4	221.0	4.2	190.1	3.6	150.8	2.8	6.8	0.1	1,111.9	20.9	5,324.5	100
Sex														
Male	3,500.4	68.3	220.4	4.3	189.7	3.7	143.9	2.8	6.0	0.1	1,063.4	20.8	5,123.7	100
Female	140.6	71.1	0.6	0.3	0.4	0.2	6.9	3.5	0.8	0.4	48.5	24.5	197.8	100
Age 17 or younger	115.4	70.0	10.7	6.5	5.4	3.3	2.8	1.7	0.0	0.0	30.5	18.5	164.9	100
18–24	850.9	67.8	52.4	4.2	52.4	4.2	39.9	3.2	1.1	0.1	258.5	20.6	1,255.2	100
25–34	1,087.1	67.4	69.4	4.3	64.7	4.0	46.0	2.9	0.9	0.1	344.1	21.3	1,612.0	100
35–44	786.3	68.0	41.6	3.6	35.5	3.1	37.3	3.2	2.2	0.2	252.7	21.9	1,155.6	100
45–54	509.5	70.5	30.0	4.2	21.1	2.9	14.6	2.0	0.8	0.1	147.1	20.3	723.3	100
55 or older	246.2	69.9	12.3	3.5	8.0	2.3	6.7	1.9	0.0	0.0	79.0	22.4	352.2	100
Unknown	48.5	79.1	4.5	7.4	3.0	5.0	3.5	5.7	1.7	2.8	0.0	0.0	61.3	100
Race/Hispanic origin														
White, non-Hispanic	1,764.9	75.0	27.9	1.2	47.4	2.0	36.5	1.5	3.2	0.1	472.5	20.1	2,352.3	100
Black, non-Hispanic	1,093.6	64.9	77.0	4.6	70.5	4.2	36.2	2.1	2.2	0.1	404.2	24.0	1,683.7	100
Hispanic, any race	581.7	59.2	89.1	9.1	56.1	5.7	54.9	5.6	1.4	0.1	199.7	20.3	982.7	100
Other	86.0	63.2	4.8	3.5	4.9	3.6	4.9	3.6	0.0	0.0	35.5	26.1	136.2	100
Unknown	117.8	69.5	22.2	13.1	11.2	6.6	18.3	10.8	0.0	0.0	0.0	0.0	169.6	100

Note: The 'AVG N' represents the mean count across all replicates.

Table 4. ARD law enforcement homicides, by matching variable and match outcome, 2003–09 and 2011

Matching variable	No match		Probability match								Certainty match		Total	
			0.01 – 0.25		0.26 – 0.50		0.51 – 0.75		0.76 – 0.99					
	AVG N	%	AVG N	%	AVG N	%	AVG N	%	AVG N	%	AVG N	%	AVG N	%
All LE homicides	1,939.5	53.6	221.0	6.1	190.1	5.3	150.8	4.2	6.8	0.2	1,111.9	30.7	3,620.0	100
Sex														
Male	1,865.7	53.5	220.4	6.3	189.7	5.4	143.9	4.1	6.0	0.2	1,063.4	30.5	3,489.0	100
Female	73.8	56.3	0.6	0.5	0.4	0.3	6.9	5.3	0.8	0.6	48.5	37.1	131.0	100
Age														
17 or younger	57.5	53.8	10.7	10.0	5.4	5.0	2.8	2.7	0.0	0.0	30.5	28.5	107.0	100
18–24	427.7	51.4	52.4	6.3	52.4	6.3	39.9	4.8	1.1	0.1	258.5	31.1	832.0	100
25–34	555.0	51.4	69.4	6.4	64.7	6.0	46.0	4.3	0.9	0.1	344.1	31.9	1,080.0	100
35–44	426.7	53.6	41.6	5.2	35.5	4.5	37.3	4.7	2.2	0.3	252.7	31.7	796.0	100
45–54	297.3	58.2	30.0	5.9	21.1	4.1	14.6	2.9	0.8	0.2	147.1	28.8	511.0	100
55 or older	143.1	57.5	12.3	4.9	8.0	3.2	6.7	2.7	0.0	0.0	79.0	31.7	249.0	100
Unknown	32.2	71.5	4.5	10.1	3.0	6.7	3.5	7.8	1.7	3.8	0.0	0.0	45.0	100
Race/Hispanic origin														
White, non-Hispanic	926.6	61.2	27.9	1.8	47.4	3.1	36.5	2.4	3.2	0.2	472.5	31.2	1,514.0	100
Black, non-Hispanic	550.8	48.3	77.0	6.8	70.5	6.2	36.2	3.2	2.2	0.2	404.2	35.4	1,141.0	100
Hispanic, any race	322.9	44.6	89.1	12.3	56.1	7.7	54.9	7.6	1.4	0.2	199.7	27.6	724.0	100
Other	45.8	47.8	4.8	5.0	4.9	5.1	4.9	5.2	0.0	0.0	35.5	37.0	96.0	100
Unknown	93.2	64.3	22.2	15.3	11.2	7.7	18.3	12.6	0.0	0.0	0.0	0.0	145.0	100

Note: The 'AVG N' represents the mean count across all replicates.

Table 5. ARD law enforcement homicide decedent characteristics, by source, 2003–09 and 2011

	Percent of all law enforcement homicide victims											
	All years			2003–06			2007–09			2011		
Decedent characteristics	ARD only	SHR only	ARD and SHR	ARD only	SHR only	ARD and SHR	ARD only	SHR only	ARD and SHR	ARD only	SHR only	ARD and SHR
Age												
17 or younger	3.0%	3.4%	2.9%	3.3%	3.2%	3.0%	3.3%	4.1%	3.5%	1.5%	1.1%	1.7%
18–24	22.1	24.8	24.1	22.2	24.9	25.1	22.0	25.3	23.8	21.9	22.2	22.5
25–34	28.6	31.2	31.2	29.3	31.4	31.4	29.0	30.6	31.5	26.3	33.6	30.2
35–44	22.0	21.1	22.0	23.4	23.3	23.6	21.1	18.9	20.8	20.3	18.0	21.0
45–54	15.3	12.5	12.7	14.2	11.2	10.5	14.5	13.3	13.4	19.9	16.2	16.0
55 or older	7.4	6.1	6.3	5.7	5.3	5.3	8.2	6.6	6.2	10.0	8.4	8.5
Unknown	1.7	1.0	0.8	2.0	0.7	1.2	2.0	1.4	0.7	0.2	0.5	0.1
Race/Hispanic origin												
White, non-Hispanic	47.8%	49.2%	35.0%	49.8%	49.9%	35.2%	43.4%	47.0%	35.3%	51.0%	55.2%	33.8%
Black, non-Hispanic	28.4	31.8	35.1	26.5	30.1	33.2	33.3	34.4	35.7	23.9	29.8	38.0
Hispanic, any race	16.7	15.2	23.9	17.1	15.9	25.5	16.2	14.6	22.5	16.3	13.3	23.2
Other	2.4	2.4	3.0	3.1	2.9	4.4	1.7	2.0	2.4	1.9	0.5	1.2
Unknown	4.8	1.4	3.1	3.5	1.1	1.8	5.4	1.9	4.1	6.9	1.2	3.7
Manner of death												
Firearm	96.3%	96.0%	97.0%	99.4%	97.0%	99.9%	90.6%	94.9%	92.5%	99.4%	94.8%	100%
Other	3.7	4.0	3.0	0.6	3.0	0.1	9.4	5.1	7.5	0.6	5.2	0.0
Missing	0.0	0.0	0.0	0.1	0.0	0.0	0.0	0.0	0.0	0.0	0.0	0.0

3.2. Variability in ARD Methodology across States

As described in Section 3.1, RTI calculated the size of the law enforcement homicide population in the United States and the ARD program coverage using two methods. The first, a simple, poststratified Lincoln-Petersen method, assumes that all nonreporting law enforcement agencies did not have any law enforcement homicides during the observation period and therefore has no agency adjustment. The second coverage estimate assumes that all nonreporting agencies have the same number of law enforcement homicides on average as agencies that did report to either the SHR or the ARD program. This poststratified Lincoln-Petersen assumes that the population of interest is closed geographically and in time and is of fixed size, with a constant ratio adjustment for unobserved agencies. Table 6 and figure 4 show coverage estimates using each method by the year observed. The highest coverage rate with no agency adjustment was found in the most recent collection year of 2011 (69%).

Table 6. ARD coverage estimates and confidence intervals, by estimation approach, 2003– 09 and 2011

	No agency adjustment			Agency adjustment		
Year	95% Lower bound	Coverage estimate	95% Upper bound	95% Lower bound	Coverage estimate	95% Upper bound
All study years	47.28%	48.70%	50.18%	34.50%	36.43%	38.35%
2003	36.87	41.84	46.82	21.96	26.61	31.27
2004	37.30	42.89	48.49	24.41	29.46	34.52
2005	33.67	38.55	43.43	19.90	24.25	28.59
2006	42.50	46.99	51.48	28.73	33.37	38.02
2007	46.45	50.51	54.58	35.18	39.61	44.04
2008	36.50	40.81	45.12	22.57	26.82	31.07
2009	51.37	54.98	58.59	35.00	39.64	44.29
2011	65.12	69.01	72.90	53.85	58.58	63.30

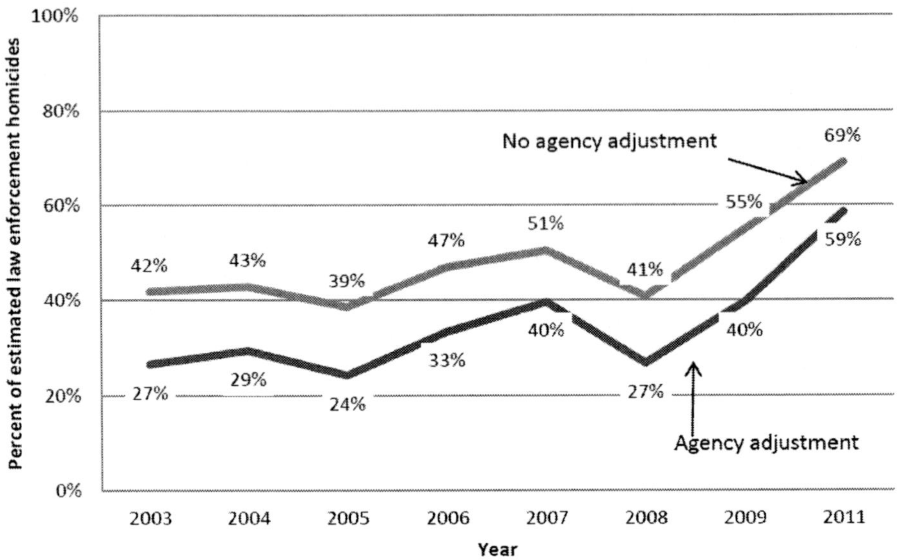

Figure 4. Percent of law enforcement homicide universe covered by ARD, by estimation method, 2003–09 and 2011.

The methodology for identifying ARD cases has changed over the observation period, and figure 4 suggests that the methods used in more recent years are associated with better coverage. To better understand the methodologies used to identify arrest-related deaths in 2011, RTI conducted interviews with state reporting coordinators (SRCs). These interviews explored the primary method each SRC used for identifying cases, whether direct reporting from law enforcement agencies was involved, and whether the SRCs conducted any sort of follow-up or verification of cases reported to them. In addition, RTI tracked information about reporting methods and SRC location throughout the 2011 data collection period. This information was used to further examine the utility of various methodologies for identifying arrest-related deaths, as implemented by the SRCs during the 2011 data collection.

The remaining analyses examine differences in case matching by state and reporting method. RTI grouped states by the primary data collection methodology and the location of the SRCs. Then, RTI conducted analyses to compare the number of cases reported only to ARD, only to SHR, or to both programs. Because the methodology for reporting was determined largely through the SRC interviews and information gained during the 2011 data collection period, these analyses are limited to 2011 data only. Table 7 describes state-level variation in reporting. In 2011, 83% of law enforcement homicides reported to either system were estimated to be captured in the ARD program. Approximately 139 of the estimated 828 law enforcement homicides captured by either system were reported only to the SHR.

There is considerable variability among states in the proportion of law enforcement homicides that are reported only to the ARD program, only to SHR, or to both sources. Three states reported to both systems but had no estimated overlap between the two (Iowa, Minnesota, and Arkansas). In other words, no law enforcement homicides reported to ARD were matched to homicides found in the SHR, and the SHR deaths were not matched to any of the ARD deaths in these three states. Twelve states reported all law enforcement homicides captured by either system to ARD: Connecticut, Massachusetts, New Hampshire, New York, Kansas, North Dakota, Alabama, Mississippi, West Virginia, Alaska, Idaho, and Montana. No states reported law enforcement homicides only to the SHR. Reporting to ARD is estimated to capture at least 75% of cases reported to either system for 38 states, 11 of which reported at least 20 law enforcement homicides to either system in 2011. Missouri, Maryland, Hawaii, and Nevada were each estimated to report more cases to the SHR than the ARD program. However, ARD still captured 82% of the estimated cases in Maryland and 84% of the cases in Nevada, and Hawaii had very few arrest-related deaths reported to either system. In Missouri, half of the cases reported to either system were found in the ARD, but 87% of the cases reported to either system were found in the SHR. Rhode Island, Vermont, Delaware, and Wyoming did not report any law enforcement homicides to either system in 2011.

3.2.1. ARD Law Enforcement Homicide Reporting Methodology

Primary data collection methodology was determined through interviews with the SRCs in 2012 and from information gathered during the 2011 data collection period (see table 8). Most states (N = 26) relied solely on media to identify ARD-eligible cases. ARD program staff identified cases in four states, also relying primarily on media sources. Eight states used direct reporting from local law enforcement agencies, and seven states relied on direct reporting from medical examiner's/coroner's offices. Four states accessed the National Violent Death Reporting System (NVDRS). Finally, two states had a legislative mandate to report arrest-related deaths.

Table 7. ARD law enforcement homicides, by region, state, and source, 2011

	ARD only			SHR only			ARD and SHR		
Region and state	AVG N	Row %	Col %	AVG N	Row %	Col %	AVG N	Row %	Col %
Total	361.3	43.6	100	139.3	16.8	100	327.7	39.6	100
Northeast	50.0	55.6	13.8	9.0	10.0	6.5	31.0	34.4	9.5
Connecticut	2.0	100	0.6	0.0	0.0	0.0	0.0	0.0	0.0
Maine	2.6	30.6	0.7	2.6	30.6	1.9	3.4	38.9	1.0
Massachusetts	5.0	100	1.4	0.0	0.0	0.0	0.0	0.0	0.0
New Hampshire	4.0	80.0	1.1	0.0	0.0	0.0	1.0	20.0	0.3
New Jersey	4.0	25.0	1.1	4.0	25.0	2.9	8.0	50.0	2.4
New York	26.0	100	7.2	0.0	0.0	0.0	0.0	0.0	0.0
Pennsylvania	6.4	23.3	1.8	2.4	8.7	1.7	18.6	68.0	5.7
Rhode Island	0.0	0.0	0.0	0.0	0.0	0.0	0.0	0.0	0.0
Vermont	0.0	0.0	0.0	0.0	0.0	0.0	0.0	0.0	0.0
Midwest	78.7	50.6	21.8	31.7	20.4	22.8	45.3	29.1	13.8
Illinois	9.1	28.4	2.5	1.1	3.4	0.8	21.9	68.2	6.7
Indiana	8.7	46.6	2.4	5.7	30.6	4.1	4.3	22.8	1.3
Iowa	4.0	80.0	1.1	1.0	20.0	0.7	0.0	0.0	0.0
Kansas	6.0	85.7	1.7	0.0	0.0	0.0	1.0	14.3	0.3
Michigan	8.0	44.4	2.2	5.0	27.8	3.6	5.0	27.8	1.5
Minnesota	2.0	50.0	0.6	2.0	50.0	1.4	0.0	0.0	0.0
Missouri	2.4	13.2	0.7	9.4	51.2	6.8	6.6	35.6	2.0
Nebraska	1.0	33.3	0.3	1.0	33.3	0.7	1.0	33.3	0.3
North Dakota	1.0	100	0.3	0.0	0.0	0.0	0.0	0.0	0.0
Ohio	29.5	88.0	8.2	0.5	1.4	0.3	3.5	10.6	1.1
South Dakota	3.0	42.9	0.8	3.0	42.9	2.2	1.0	14.3	0.3

	ARD only			SHR only			ARD and SHR		
Region and state	AVG N	Row %	Col %	AVG N	Row %	Col %	AVG N	Row %	Col %
Wisconsin	4.0	50.0	1.1	3.0	37.5	2.2	1.0	12.5	0.3
South	125.8	41.0	34.8	52.8	17.2	37.9	128.2	41.8	39.1
Alabama	7.0	100	1.9	0.0	0.0	0.0	0.0	0.0	0.0
Arkansas	3.0	75.0	0.8	1.0	25.0	0.7	0.0	0.0	0.0
Delaware	0.0	0.0	0.0	0.0	0.0	0.0	0.0	0.0	0.0
District of Columbia	0.4	6.6	0.1	0.4	6.6	0.3	4.6	86.8	1.4
Florida	20.8	24.2	5.8	19.8	23.1	14.2	45.2	52.7	13.8
Georgia	12.9	43.1	3.6	3.9	13.0	2.8	13.1	43.8	4.0
Kentucky	8.0	61.5	2.2	3.0	23.1	2.2	2.0	15.4	0.6
Louisiana	3.7	42.8	1.0	1.7	20.0	1.3	3.3	37.2	1.0
Maryland	2.8	13.4	0.8	3.8	18.2	2.7	14.2	68.3	4.3
Mississippi	7.0	87.5	1.9	0.0	0.0	0.0	1.0	12.5	0.3
North Carolina	12.0	80.0	3.3	1.0	6.7	0.7	2.0	13.3	0.6
Oklahoma	5.1	31.5	1.4	3.1	19.1	2.2	7.9	49.4	2.4
South Carolina	5.4	52.1	1.5	3.4	32.9	2.5	1.6	15.0	0.5
Tennessee	2.1	15.8	0.6	2.1	15.8	1.5	8.9	68.5	2.7
Texas	23.1	47.1	6.4	7.1	14.5	5.1	18.9	38.4	5.8
Virginia	10.5	56.8	2.9	2.5	13.6	1.8	5.5	29.6	1.7
West Virginia	2.0	100	0.6	0.0	0.0	0.0	0.0	0.0	0.0
West	106.7	38.7	29.5	45.7	16.6	32.8	123.3	44.7	37.6
Alaska	1.0	50.0	0.3	0.0	0.0	0.0	1.0	50.0	0.3
Arizona	5.0	21.7	1.4	3.0	13.0	2.1	15.0	65.3	4.6

Table 7. (Continued)

Region and state	ARD only			SHR only			ARD and SHR		
	AVG N	Row %	Col %	AVG N	Row %	Col %	AVG N	Row %	Col %
California	52.7	34.7	14.6	27.7	18.3	19.9	71.3	47.0	21.8
Colorado	10.1	59.1	2.8	5.1	29.8	3.7	1.9	11.1	0.6
Hawaii	0.1	4.4	0.0	2.1	68.1	1.5	0.9	27.4	0.3
Idaho	3.0	100	0.8	0.0	0.0	0.0	0.0	0.0	0.0
Montana	2.0	100	0.6	0.0	0.0	0.0	0.0	0.0	0.0
Nevada	1.6	9.4	0.4	2.6	15.4	1.8	12.4	75.2	3.8
New Mexico	5.9	49.4	1.6	1.9	15.6	1.3	4.1	35.0	1.3
Oregon	3.2	61.7	0.9	0.2	4.3	0.2	1.8	33.9	0.5
Utah	2.6	39.4	0.7	1.6	24.3	1.1	2.4	36.3	0.7
Washington	19.6	58.3	5.4	1.6	4.7	1.1	12.4	37.0	3.8
Wyoming	0.0	0.0	0.0	0.0	0.0	0.0	0.0	0.0	0.0

Note: These are the mean counts across all replicates.

Table 8. Primary methodology for identifying arrest-related deaths, by state, 2011

Legislative mandate	Direct law enforcement agency report	Direct medical examiner's/ coroner's report	National Violent Death Reporting System	Media only		Arrest-Related Death Program staff
CA	AL	CO	KY	AK	MN	AR
TX	DC	ME	OK	AZ	NE	GA
	KS	MA	OR	CT	NY	WI
	MO	NM	UT	DE	NJ	WY
	NH	NC		FL	ND	
	NV	SC		HI	OH	
	TN	WA		ID	PA	
	VT			IL	RI	
				IN	SD	
				IA	VA	
				LA	WV	
				MD	MS	
				MI	MT	

Note: States are listed using standard U.S. postal abbreviations.

Figure 5 shows that there was not much variability in the proportion of observed law enforcement homicides that were found in the ARD program based on the primary identification method. The proportion of observed cases found in ARD ranged from a low of 80% for states that relied primarily on direct law enforcement agency reports to a high of 85% for states that relied on reports from medical examiner's or coroner's offices. The lack of association between the primary identification method and the proportion of cases found in ARD could be due to imprecise methods for categorizing states. For example, there may be additional variability within primary methodologies. Some states with direct law enforcement agency reports may have received these from only a few agencies in the state, and without a backup form of identification, were missing many law enforcement homicides. The majority of states relied on media reports, but there was likely to be considerable variability in the number of media sources reviewed, whether such review was proactive or reactive, and whether media-identified reports were then verified. Furthermore, the information RTI received about primary identification methodology may not have reflected the true methods that the SRC uses in that state, due to incomplete or outdated information collected during the SRC interviews or during the 2011 data collection period.

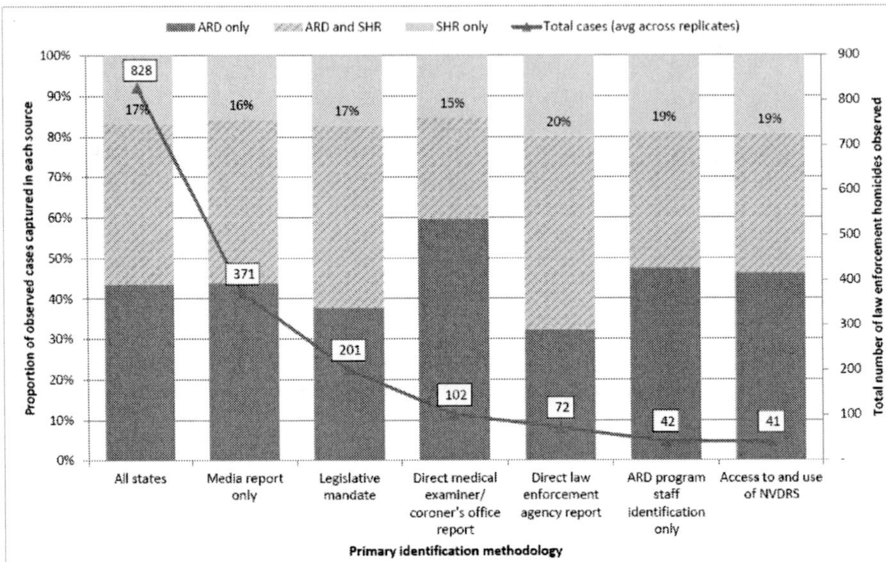

Figure 5. Law enforcement homicides, by source and primary reporting method, 2011.

3.2.2. Location of SRC

States were also categorized by the location of the SRC. The greatest number of SRCs (25) were located in a planning, commission, or statistics agency, such as a statistical analysis center, a research or data agency within the state's department of criminal justice, or a planning organization (see table 9). SRCs in 13 states were situated in a state-level law enforcement or public safety department. There were three SRCs in a state prosecutor's office, three in a medical examiner/coroner's office or health agency, and three in a state corrections agency.

Figure 6 describes the proportion of observed law enforcement homicides that were found in ARD by SRC location. SRCs located in state prosecutors' offices and statistical analysis or other research centers, and those located in "other" locations, each had approximately 87% of the observed cases found in ARD, and only 13% of the observed cases found only in SHR. SRCs located in state law enforcement agencies and state corrections agencies had the lowest proportion of observed cases found in ARD (76% and 75%, respectively). State law enforcement agencies may not have collected data regularly from local law enforcement agencies to report to ARD, or they may have captured data only from a subset of agencies in the state. Data reported to the SHR, on the other hand, came directly from local law enforcement agencies. SRCs located in state corrections agencies may not have had the direct access or necessary relationships to regularly collect information on law enforcement homicides that occurred during the process of arrest. Further analysis may be warranted to determine how staff in state law enforcement agencies work with local agencies to identify and collect information about law enforcement homicides.

Table 9. SRC agency location, 2011

State law enforcement agency or public safety dept	State prosecutors office	Medical examiner/ coroner's office or health agency	State corrections agency	Planning, commission, or statistics agency		Arrest-Related Death programs taff
CO	NH	ME	ID	AK	NM	AR
FL	ND	NC	IN	AZ	NY	GA
HI	TX	OR	LA	CA	OH	WI
MA				CT	OK	WY
MI				DE	PA	
MN				IL	UT	
MO				IA	VT	
RI				KS	VA	
SC				KY	WV	
SD				MD	AL	
TN				NV	MS	
WA				NE	MT	
DC				NJ		

Note: States are listed using standard U.S. postal abbreviations.

3.3. Number of Years at Least One Death Was Reported to ARD and SHR

Table 10 describes the number of agencies reporting at least one death for the 8 years observed in these analyses, and the estimated number of deaths reported by those agencies. Overall, more unique agencies reported to ARD in the years observed, 2003 through 2009 and 2011 (N = 1,261), compared to SHR (N = 881). For both systems, the majority of these unique agencies reported a death in only 1 of the 8 years examined. Fifteen agencies reported at least 1 death to ARD in all 8 years, and 28 agencies reported at least 1 death to

SHR in all 8 years. The number of unique agencies reporting deaths in 7 or 8 years is higher for the SHR system compared to the ARD program. This finding suggests that the SHR is more likely to include data from agencies that consistently have at least one law enforcement homicide each year, as compared to the ARD program. Agencies that do not have law enforcement homicides each year are more likely to be found in the ARD data.

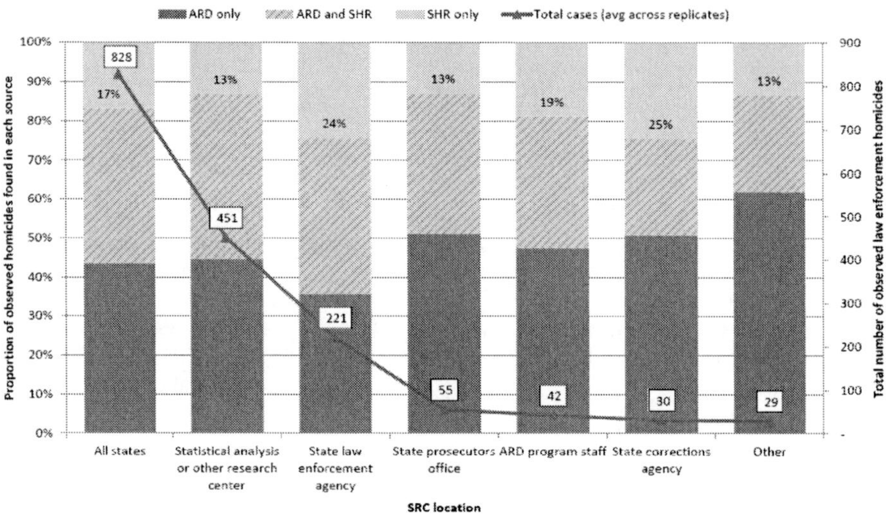

Figure 6. Law enforcement homicides, by source and SRC location, 2011.

Table 10. Number of years at least one death was reported to ARD and SHR

Number of years at least one death was reported	ARD		SHR	
	Number of agencies	Number of deaths	Number of agencies	Number of deaths
Total	1,261	3,620	881	3,385
8	15	696	28	1075
7	13	348	17	368
6	23	278	20	240
5	23	262	18	149
4	42	273	40	304
3	81	358	77	295
2	189	478	167	401
1	875	927	514	553

4. Conclusions and Recommendations

The capture-recapture analysis described above estimates that, at best, the Arrest-Related Deaths (ARD) program captured approximately half of all law enforcement homicides in the United States during the study period (2003–09, 2011). This estimate assumes that all unobserved law enforcement agencies had zero law enforcement homicides. If those unobserved agencies did have a similar number of law enforcement homicides as those that did report to the ARD program or the Supplementary Homicide Reports (SHRs), the ARD coverage estimate is reduced to 36%. This information alone may be sufficient for BJS to determine whether to continue the ARD data collection program. Additional considerations for BJS to explore regarding continuing data collection through the ARD program are described below.

4.1. Relative Strengths and Weaknesses of the ARD Program Methodology

A primary strength of the ARD program is that it was the only data collection that attempted to enumerate all arrest-related deaths in the United States. Unlike the SHR, or any other national- or state-level database, it also included accidental and natural deaths that occurred during the process of arrest in addition to law enforcement homicides. Although the current analyses did not identify any specific program methodologies that were more likely to identify law enforcement homicides than others, we did not examine their utility for identifying other types of arrest-related deaths.

4.1.1. Types of Cases That Were Covered Well by the ARD Program

Analyses of decedent characteristics did not reveal any meaningful differences in capture rates by age, sex, or race/Hispanic origin. The 2011 data collection year did exhibit some differences across decedent characteristics compared to previous years, but these differences were not confined to cases found only in the ARD program.

4.1.2. Identification Approaches That Are Associated with Better Coverage

The analyses described above did not identify specific methodologies that were associated with increased coverage. There was little variation in the percentage of observed cases found in ARD (as opposed to the SHR) based on the primary methodology employed by the SRCs. For example, our analyses indicated that 20% of all observed homicides were found only in the SHR for states where the SRC relied primarily on direct reports from law enforcement agencies to identify homicides. In other words, ARD captured 80% of the observed homicides in these states. Eighty-five percent of the observed law enforcement homicides in states that relied primarily on data from medical examiner's or coroner's offices were found in the ARD program. Among these states, 15% of the cases observed in 2011 were found only in the SHR. Examining state-level variations in reporting and matching those directly to the time put in by the SRC, the location of the SRC, and the primary identification methodology will likely shed more light on effective identification practices. BJS may also further examine the policies and practices in California and Texas. Both states have mandated reporting legislation, but our analysis suggests that approximately a fifth of the observed cases in California in 2011 were reported to the SHR only, while 14% of the observed cases in Texas in 2011 were reported to the SHR only.

4.2. Recommendations

While the capture-recapture analysis estimated that approximately half of all law enforcement homicides were not captured in the ARD program during the study period, the estimated rate of coverage for ARD in 2009 and 2011 was higher than the earlier years examined. In 2003, we estimated that the ARD program captured, at best, 42% of the universe of law enforcement homicides in the United States. In 2011, that coverage estimate increased to 69%. However, the analyses described above did not uncover any significant variations in coverage for observed homicides based on the location of the SRC or the primary identification methodology used in 2011. It is possible that all of the states were using more rigorous methodologies in 2011 as compared to earlier data collection years. Even states that relied primarily on media to identify cases may have been applying a comprehensive and regular approach to identifying these cases and following up with other agencies to verify the death. In fact, most states relied on multiple approaches to identify cases, but only the primary method was analyzed in this report.

In general, more of the observed law enforcement homicides in 2011 were found in the ARD program compared to the SHR. There was still considerable state-to-state variation in reporting to one or both programs, however, and our analyses failed to identify specific reasons for this variation, such as the SRC's location or the primary identification methodology used.

A combination of data from both the SHR and the ARD is estimated to capture, at best, 72% of all law enforcement homicides in the United States across all years observed. In 2011, the ARD program captured, at most, an estimated 69% of the universe. Despite demonstrated improvements in the ARD program coverage over time, there are still a large number of law enforcement homicides that go unreported, indicating that the ARD is not a census.

A first step to increasing the coverage of ARD is to define a consistent data collection approach across states, as opposed to the variable SRC-driven data collection methodology employed in 2011. More guidance or even requirements for where the SRC is located, how cases are identified, and verification processes may increase the reliability and coverage of the program. However, such an approach would increase the burden of this voluntary program, and would need to be balanced with the utility of the data for data providers and stakeholders at both the national and the local level.

The analyses described above only examined one alternative source for identifying law enforcement homicides. BJS may further study other potential alternatives to the SRC-focused data collection methodology to determine if any provide more cost-effective or more valid and reliable means of identifying arrest-related deaths, including primary data collection or secondary analyses of existing data sources.

Primary data collection methods such as direct surveys of law enforcement agencies or medical examiner's/coroner's offices could identify law enforcement homicides and the circumstances surrounding those homicides in the jurisdictions surveyed. Direct surveys would involve an additional burden than the ARD program's SRC-focused approach through the cost of fielding the study and the time required to collect the data, as well as the burden on survey respondents. If the survey has a sufficient response rate and demonstrated validity, however, it may be an accurate measure of law enforcement homicides in the United States.

Less burdensome methodologies could include data collection from open sources. Open sources are publicly available data compiled through targeted searches, such as Google Alerts and review of specific websites devoted to law enforcement homicides. Open sources also include public documents such as press releases from states' attorney general offices, medical examiners, or state police agencies. For example, the New York City Police Department releases an annual report describing all law enforcement homicides in that jurisdiction.

Finally, fee-based services such as www.webclipping.com can be used to identify information from a large number of media outlets. Reliance on open source methods, while cost-effective, has a number of limitations. For example, media sources are often limited to "newsworthy" deaths and may be biased toward higher profile cases. Furthermore, there may be considerable regional and local variation in media coverage for law enforcement homicide-related events. Google Alerts and web-clipping services are also constrained by the search terms provided, which must be balanced to include all potentially eligible law enforcement homicides while not resulting in an unmanageable number of "alerts" to review. The timeliness of open source searches presents another limitation, because information on web-based news platforms may be available for a limited time. Most importantly, however, the quality of information from open sources is unknown, and the accuracy, reliability, and type of content provided is likely to vary over time, by source, and in comparison to official records.

Other alternative measures of law enforcement homicides include existing data maintained by the Federal Bureau of Investigation (FBI) and the Centers for Disease Control and Prevention (CDC). Supplementary Homicide Reports (SHRs) are collected nationally as part of the FBI's Uniform Crime Reporting Program (UCR), where information is voluntarily provided by law enforcement agencies to their state UCR programs and then to the FBI. The SHR has the potential to identify or confirm ARD cases categorized as a "homicide by law enforcement officer(s)." Other publicly available data sources that may also measure law enforcement homicides include the FBI's National Incident Based Reporting System (NIBRS), and CDC's National Vital Statistics System (NVSS) and its National Violent Death Reporting System (NVDRS) Each of these data sources has known limitations. For example, data from NIBRS, NVDRS, and local law enforcement agency websites are not national in scope, and are available only for certain jurisdictions. Data from the SHR and NVSS are national in scope, but do not contain unique identifiers that would allow precise case-level matching and comparison with the cases submitted to the ARD program. Studies have further documented inconsistencies in reporting to the ARD, SHR, and NVSS both within and across states (Loftin et al., 2003; Mumola, 2007; RTI International, 2012). The ability of any of these systems to accurately capture the universe of all arrest-related deaths as defined by the ARD program, or law enforcement homicides in particular, is currently unknown.

4.3. Study Limitations

The findings described above have several limitations, some of which may be addressed in additional analyses as indicated by BJS. First, the study is limited by the approach to including all probable and certainty matches in the analyses reported in exhibits 8, 10, 12, and 14. BJS may choose to limit the cases identified as a match to those with a probability score cutoff of 0.50 or higher, or to limit them to certainty matches only. The analyses presented here represent the "best case scenario" for ARD; any assumption changes will lower the number and proportion of observed cases that overlap across the two systems and increase the number and proportion of observed cases found in one system only.

The most significant limitation of this study, however, is measurement discrepancies between the SHR and ARD on matching variables, and the lack of a unique identifier to positively link cases across the systems. The monte carlo replicate approach implemented here provides the most rigorous means of addressing this limitation, but the shortcomings in the matching variable measurement remain. Findings were presented here as estimates of "cases," but all estimates are based on the replicate approach, so any conclusions about the actual number of cases matched or covered by either system are not warranted. Instead, we can only estimate the level of matching and overlap across the two systems based on the information provided.

References

Boriah, S., Chandola, V., & Kumar, V. 2008. Similarity measures for categorical data: A comparative evaluation. In proceedings of the eighth SIAM International Conference on Data Mining. 243–254.

Loftin, C., Wiersema, B., McDowall, D. & Dobrin, A. (2003). Underreporting of justifiable homicides committed by police officers in the United States, 1976–1998. *American Journal of Public Health, 93*(7), 1117–1121.

Mumola, C.J. (2007). *Arrest-related deaths in the United States, 2003–2005.* Bureau of Justice Statistics Special Report. (NCJ 219534). Washington, DC: U.S. Department of Justice, Office of Justice Programs. Retrieved from http://bjs.ojp.usdoj.gov/index.cfm?ty=pbdetail&iid=379.

RTI International. (May 2012). Arrest-related deaths program: Program assessment, alternative approaches to data collection, and recommendations for program enhancement. Draft report submitted to the

Bureau of Justice Statistics. Washington, DC: U.S. Department of Justice, Office of Justice Programs.
Wolter, K.M. (1986). Some coverage error models for census data. *Journal of the American Statistical Association, 81* (394): 338–346.

APPENDIX A: SIMILARITY SCORING FOR ARD/SHR MATCHING INTRODUCTION

Introduction

Calculation of similarity scores in the context of matching data from the Arrest-Related Deaths (ARD) program with the Supplemental Homicide Reports (SHRs) requires a method that accounts for both continuous and categorical variables. Cases will be matched between data sources and within the originating agency identifier (ORI) code and victim sex on three measures: date of incident/date of death, age, and race/Hispanic origin, with the first two measures being continuous and the latter categorical. Given this mix of variables, RTI proposes calculating scores using a mixture of methods as follows.

Continuous Variables

For the date and age variables, we propose use of a standardized Euclidean distance, combined with a similarity transformation.

Let

N_{SHR} = number of records in SHR (within a given year)

N_{ARD} = number of records in ARD (within a given year)

i = SHR record index where $i \in [1, N_{SHR}]$

j = ARD record index where $j \in [1, N_{ARD}]$

$d_{SHR,i}$ = SHR date (measured in number of days since January 1, 1960[5]) for record i

$d_{ARD,j}$ = ARD date (measured in number of days since January 1, 1960) for record j

$a_{SHR,i}$ = SHR age for record i

$a_{ARD,j}$ = ARD age for record j

$$\acute{d}_{SHR,i} = \frac{d_{SHR,i} - mean(d_{ARD})}{std(d_{ARD})}$$

$$\acute{d}_{ARD,j} = \frac{d_{ARD,j} - mean(d_{ARD})}{std(d_{ARD})}$$

$$\acute{a}_{SHR,i} = \frac{a_{SHR,i} - mean(a_{ARD})}{std(a_{ARD})}$$

$$\acute{a}_{ARD,j} = \frac{a_{ARD,j} - mean(a_{ARD})}{std(a_{ARD})}$$

Then the standardized Euclidean distance between records i and j on date and age is given by

$$D_{i,j} = \sqrt{\left(\acute{d}_{SHR,i} - \acute{d}_{ARD,j}\right)^2 + \left(\acute{a}_{SHR,i} - \acute{a}_{ARD,j}\right)^2}$$

This distance is then transformed to a similarity score as

$$S_{con;i,j} = \frac{1}{1 + D_{i,j}}$$

where

$$0 < S_{con;i,j} \leq 1$$

Categorical Variables

Rather than simply counting matches on categorical variables as 1 and mismatches as 0, we propose the use of a penalized scoring approach similar to that described in Boriah et al., 2008.[6] This approach is based on the premise that matches that have a high probability of occurring by random chance should not count as much as those that would be observed very rarely by chance alone. For each categorical variable (currently only race/Hispanic origin), the similarity between two records i and j is given by the following.

Let

$\hat{p}(x)$ = the sample probability that $X = x$

Then the similarity between records *i* and *j* on variable *X* is given by

$$S_X = \begin{cases} 1 - \hat{p}(x_{SHR})\hat{p}(x_{ARD}) & \text{if } x_{SHR} = x_{ARD} \\ 0 & \text{otherwise} \end{cases}$$

$$0 \leq S_X < 1$$

Calculating the Overall Score

The final similarity score for records *i* and *j* is the weighted mean of the various components and is given by the following:

$$S_{i,j} = \frac{2}{3}S_{con;i,j} + \frac{1}{3}S_{RACE/ETH;i,j}$$

APPENDIX B: LINKING ALGORITHM

Estimate the Agency Population Size and Agency Undercoverage Adjustment Factor

To ensure that coverage estimates apply to the population of law enforcement (LE) homicides across all agencies and not only to the population of LE homicides occurring in agencies that have been observed, we must estimate the total population size of agencies with LE homicides (reported or unreported). To achieve this, we will use the Lincoln-Petersen (LP) estimator[7] as follows:

$$(1)\ \hat{N} = \frac{(n_{ARD}+1)(n_{SHR}+1)}{n_{ARD||SHR}+1} - 1$$

In (1), n_{ARD} is the number of agencies in ARD, n_{SHR} is the number of agencies in SHR, and $n_{ARD||SHR}$ is the number of agencies represented in both sources. The variance of $\widehat{N}$ is given by the following:

$$(2)\quad Var(\widehat{N}) = \frac{(n_{ARD}+1)(n_{SHR}+1)(n_{ARD}-n_{ARD||SHR})(n_{SHR}-n_{ARD||SHR})}{n^2_{ARD||SHR}(n_{ARD||SHR}+2)}$$

The number of agencies observed across ARD and SHR is given by

$$n = n_{ARD} + n_{SHR} - n_{ARD||SHR}$$

and the agency undercoverage adjustment factor is given by

$$R = \frac{\widehat{N}}{n}$$

and its variance is given by

$$Var(R) = \frac{Var(\widehat{N})}{n^2}$$

Classify Cases as Matchable or Unmatchable

For the purposes of record linkage, cases are separated into two groups determined by whether or not it is possible to match them between sources, within characteristic classifications that must be the same: originating agency identifier (ORI) code, sex, and year. Cases from either source that cannot be matched on these three characteristics are considered unmatchable and are excluded from subsequent probabilistic linking.

Probabilistic Linking between ARD and SHR

For cases considered matchable across sources, probabilistic linking is used to determine whether a case in the Arrest-Related Deaths (ARD) program is the same as a case in the Supplementary Homicide Reports (SHRs). Within each distinct combination of ORI, sex, and year, probabilistic linking proceeds according to the following steps:

a. Randomly sort the ARD cases

b. For each ARD case i, calculate a similarity score, $S_{i,j}$, corresponding to each SHR case j

c. Create a 0/1 indicator, $u_{i,j}$, indicating whether SHR case j has already been linked to another ARD record

d. Define $S'_{i,j} = S_{i,j} * (1 - u_{i,j})$

e. Create a 0/1 indicator, $t_{i,j}$, for whether or not each SHR case is within acceptable threshold for being considered the same as the ARD case in question (an SHR case is considered within threshold if the difference in dates of incident and death is less than or equal to 30 days, the ages are less than or equal to 5 years apart, and the race/Hispanic origin matches exactly); Note that if $u_{i,j} = 1$ then $t_{i,j} = 0$

f. Treating the scores as unscaled probabilities, calculate the probability that the ARD case is not represented in SHR as follows

$$S_{i,none} = \prod_{j=1}^{k} (1 - S'_{i,j})\,(1 - t_{i,j})$$

g. Determine the number of cases that are within threshold as

$$n_t = \sum_{j=1}^{k} t_{i,j}$$

h. If $n_t > 0$ then define $S''_{i,j} = S'_{i,j} * t_{i,j}$

i. Otherwise, if $n_t = 0$, then define $S''_{i,j} = S'_{i,j}$

j. Define $p_{i,j}$, the probability that ARD case i is the same as SHR case j as

$$p_{i,j} = \frac{S''_{i,j}}{S_{i,none} + \sum_1^j S''_{i,j}}$$

k. Define the probability of no match as

$$p_{i,none} = \frac{S_{i,none}}{S_{i,none} + \sum_{1}^{j} S''_{i,j}}$$

l. Define the cumulative probability of record linkage as

$$c_{i,j} = \sum_{q=1}^{j} p_{i,q}$$

m. Select a random variate x_i, from $X \sim UNIFORM(0,1)$

n. Link ARD case *i* with SHR case *j* if case *j* is the first case (going from 1 to *k*) such that $c_{i,j} > x_i$

o. If this condition is not satisfied, ARD case *i* will be linked to no SHR cases with probability $p_{i,none}$

Recombine Cases

Once matchable cases have gone through the probabilistic linking process, they are recombined with cases previously determined to be unmatchable due to a lack of overlap on key variables (ORI, sex, and year). Once recombined, the number of individual homicides in ARD, in SHR, and in both ARD and SHR are tabulated; these are denoted as m_{ARD}, m_{SHR}, and $m_{\text{ARD}||\text{SHR}}$, respectively.

Stratify by Individual-Level Characteristics

Since homogeneity of capture probabilities cannot be assumed within or across lists, the LP estimator of population size may contain downward bias, leading to an overestimation of coverage (Wolter, 1986). A common method for amelioration of this bias—and the one we employ—is poststratification. Once record linkage has occurred, cases will be grouped into *s* strata, defined by the cross-classification of demographic characteristics. If these characteristics are correlated with capture probability, bias incurred through use of the LP estimator will be reduced – the choice of characteristics is limited to information available in both sources (age, race/Hispanic origin, and sex).

Estimate population size and Variance by Stratum

Within each stratum l, with $1 \leq l \leq s$, obtain the LP estimate of population size and its associated variance as

$$(3)\quad \widehat{M}_l = \frac{(m_{l,ARD}+1)(m_{l,SHR}+1)}{m_{l,ARD||SHR}+1} - 1$$

The variance of $\widehat{M}_l$ is given by the following:

$$(4)\quad Var(\widehat{M}_l) = \frac{(m_{l,ARD}+1)(m_{l,SHR}+1)(m_{l,ARD}-m_{l,ARD||SHR})(m_{l,SHR}-m_{l,ARD||SHR}}{m^2_{l,ARD||SHR}(m_{l,ARD||SHR}+2)}$$

Estimate Population Size

By summing the stratum-specific population sizes, we obtain the overall population size among observed agencies:

$$\widehat{M} = \sum_{l=1}^{s} \widehat{M}_l$$

The variance of $\widehat{M}$ is given by the following:

$$Var(\widehat{M}) = \sum_{l=1}^{s} Var(\widehat{M}_l)$$

Adjust Population Size for Agency Undercoverage

To obtain an estimate of the overall population size, $\widehat{P}$, among all agencies with LE homicides, including those unobserved across lists, we apply the ratio from 1 as follows:

$$\hat{P} = R * \hat{M}$$

The variance of $\hat{P}$ is given by the following:

$$Var(\hat{P}) = \hat{M}^2 Var(R) + R^2 Var(\hat{M})$$

Estimate ARD Coverage

ARD coverage is estimated as the number of cases observed in ARD, divided by the estimated population size:

$$(5) \quad C = \frac{m_{ARD}}{\hat{P}}$$

The variance of C is given by the following:

$$(6) \quad Var(C) = \frac{C^2}{\hat{P}^2} * Var(\hat{P})$$

Replication

To achieve final estimates of coverage and variance that take into account uncertainty inherent to the probabilistic record linkage, the process above is repeated 1,000 times. In each of these replicates the linking procedure yields different results, and this variability is incorporated as follows:

Let r be the replicate index, where $1 \leq r \leq 1{,}000$, then the overall population size estimate is given by

$$\hat{P} = \frac{1}{1{,}000} \sum_{r=1}^{1{,}000} \hat{P}_r$$

The variance of $\hat{P}$ is given by the following:

$$Var(\hat{P}) = \frac{1}{1{,}000} \left[\sum_{r=1}^{1{,}000} Var(\hat{P}_r) \right] + \frac{1}{999} \left[\sum_{r=1}^{1{,}000} (\hat{P}_r - \hat{P})^2 \right]$$

The final coverage estimate and variance are obtained by replacing $\hat{P}$ and $Var(\hat{P})$ with the above in equations (5) and (6), respectively.

APPENDIX C: RACE/HISPANIC ORIGIN CODING

Before matching and capture-recapture analyses may begin, RTI must recode race/Hispanic origin to be comparable between the Arrest-Related Deaths (ARD) program and Supplementary Homicide Report (SHR) data sources. This requirement presents a problem in that race/Hispanic origin is collected in a combined measure for the ARD and in two separate variables for the SHR. Since separating the combined ARD measure into two variables comparable to those that exist in the SHR would yield a missing race for all records currently coded as Hispanic, it is much more desirable to create a combined measure on the SHR file that is comparable to that in the ARD data. Given high levels of missingness in the SHR Hispanic origin measure, this approach is also not without problems.

Hispanic Origin in the SHR

At the national level, Hispanic origin in the SHR is highly underreported, with a missingness rate of 53% in the years 2003–11.

V22	Frequency	Percent	Cumulative Frequency
	2051	53.44	2051
(H) Hispanic origin	600	15.63	2651
(N) Not of Hispanic origin	1101	28.69	3752
(U) Unknown or not reported	86	2.24	3838

To examine whether SHR respondents may be using the Hispanic origin variable as an extra race category, when needed (i.e., when the deceased was obviously Hispanic), we explored the hypothesis that if the Hispanic origin responses that were not missing were mostly 1, it would be a strong indication that this was true. As shown in the frequency above, this is not the case. So, we dug a little deeper to see where the missing Hispanic origin cases were coming from, with the following result:

State N Reported Hisp.

ƒƒƒƒƒƒƒƒƒƒƒƒƒƒƒƒƒƒƒƒƒƒƒƒƒƒƒƒƒƒƒƒƒƒƒ

State	N	Reported Hisp.
ALA	10	0
ALASKA	18	0
ARIZ	177	0.8983051
ARK	16	0
GA	82	0.4512195
HAWAII	8	0
IDAHO	3	0
ILL	137	0
IND	50	0
IOWA	17	0
KANS	14	0
KY	19	0
LA	65	0
MAINE	18	0
MASS	11	0
MD	169	0
MICH	78	0.1153846
MINN	31	0
MISS	2	0
MO	103	0.6116505
MONT	7	0
N C	42	0.7619048
N DAK	1	0
N H	2	0
N J	102	0
CALIF	993	0.9073515
[redacted]		
CONN	4	0
D C	17	0
DEL	1	0
[redacted]		
N Y	53	0
NEBR	11	0.1818182
[redacted]		
OHIO	44	0
OKLA	92	0.5978261
OREG	33	0.6666667
PA	185	0.9621622
R I	1	0
S C	20	0
S DAK	7	0
TENN	73	0
TEXAS	320	0.8937500
UTAH	23	0
V I	3	0
VA	45	0
VT	3	0
W VA	2	0
WASH	98	0.2346939
WIS	47	0.4255319
WYO	3	0

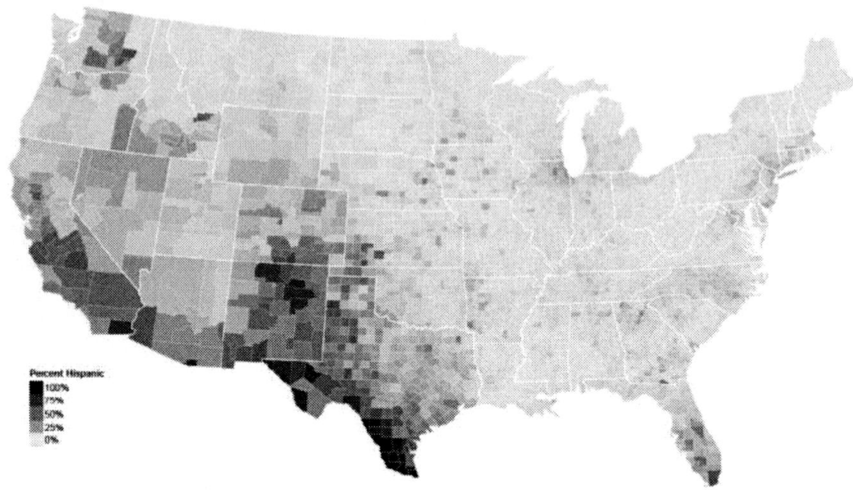

Figure 7. ACS 5-year Hispanic origin, by county.

Highlighted in the table at left are the states where we would expect to find the largest Hispanic populations. Of the 2,068 cases occurring in these states, 72% come from states with high Hispanic origin coverage. This implies that the situation may not be as bad at the national level as it might seem based only on the frequency above.

Assuming we were to create a combined race/Hispanic origin variable for the SHR, the distribution of white, black, and Hispanic nationally in 2003–09 would be 45.89%, 33.89%, and 16.28%, respectively. In the ARD, the corresponding breakdown is 42.06%, 31.03%, and 20.36%.

If we subset to states with reporting rates for Hispanic origin greater than 75% (Arizona, California, North Carolina, Pennsylvania, and Texas), the SHR distribution of white, black, and Hispanic becomes 35.54%, 25.20%, and 34.01%, respectively. The corresponding breakdown in the ARD, when subset to the same states, is 32.38%, 26.39%, and 34.70%.

Given these results, we follow an approach in which we create a combined race/Hispanic origin measure in the SHR and conduct both a national analysis as well as one subset to the states with high Hispanic origin reporting. Using only these five states would cover half of our national sample and would give us some insight into how sensitive the capture-recapture results are to the issue of data regarding Hispanic origin.

End Notes

[1] The SHR homicide also includes a small number of law enforcement-related homicides that are not classified as justifiable, but those cases cannot be identified.

[2] Age values in the SHR are considered imprecise and have been observed to clump around 5-year marks. Additionally, the SHR date is the month and year the homicide was reported. These factors necessitate a certain level of leeway in the criteria for linking and are what drive the linking threshold definitions.

[3] As part of the data quality checks, the ARD files were sorted several ways (i.e., state, year, name, date of death, and date of birth) to identify duplicate records. This method was successful in identifying duplicate entries even when the decedent had different names listed (e.g., first and last name inverted or middle name used as last name). In addition, every ARD case was cross-referenced with the DCRP Jails file to identify duplicates across DCRP collections. BJS used a similar method with the SHR file and removed any duplicates identified.

[4] Use of a simple, unstratified LP estimator likely results in deflationary bias in the law enforcement homicide agency population estimate; its use is necessitated by resource constraints that precluded collection and inclusion of agency-level characteristics for poststratification.

[5] The midpoint of the reported SHR month will be used to calculate the number of days since January 1, 1960, the standard date convention used by SAS statistical software.

[6] The proposed method is similar to the *Goodall3* approach described by Boriah et al., but adapted for two data sources.

[7] By incorporating agency-level characteristics into a stratified LP estimate, we may reduce bias induced by the assumption that agencies are observed with constant probability across agency characteristics.

INDEX

A

access, 38, 67
adjustment, 47, 48, 49, 50, 51, 55, 59, 77
age, 1, 4, 40, 41, 47, 51, 54, 55, 69, 74, 75, 80
agencies, 2, 5, 14, 16, 18, 19, 20, 22, 23, 30, 32, 33, 34, 35, 37, 38, 39, 45, 46, 47, 48, 49, 50, 59, 60, 61, 65, 66, 67, 68, 69, 70, 71, 72, 76, 77, 80, 81, 86
Alaska, 6, 7, 8, 9, 10, 12, 14, 15, 17, 61, 63
algorithm, 43, 44
arrest, vii, 1, 2, 3, 4, 5, 6, 7, 8, 9, 11, 13, 14, 16, 17, 18, 19, 20, 21, 22, 23, 24, 27, 28, 29, 30, 32, 33, 34, 35, 37, 38, 55, 60, 61, 65, 67, 69, 71, 72
arson, 17, 18
assault, 4, 17, 18
assessment, 27, 29, 30, 31, 35, 37, 38, 39, 73

B

benefits, 45, 48
bias, 44, 45, 46, 48, 79, 85, 86
bounds, 36, 47
breakdown, 85
Bureau of Justice Statistics (BJS), vii, 1, 2, 4, 11, 12, 14, 21, 22, 23, 24, 27, 28, 29, 30, 31, 32, 33, 34, 35, 37, 38, 46, 49, 69, 70, 71, 73, 74, 85

C

cation, 9, 19, 20
CDC, 22, 72
census, 16, 19
certificate, 22
child maltreatment, 34
classification, 42, 46, 80
convention, 86
cost, 71, 72
covering, 29

D

data collection, 21, 23, 29, 30, 34, 35, 36, 37, 38, 60, 61, 66, 69, 70, 71, 73
data set, 39
database, 69
DEA, 22
deaths, vii, 1, 2, 3, 4, 5, 6, 7, 8, 9, 11, 12, 13, 14, 16, 17, 18, 19, 20, 21, 22, 23, 24, 27, 28, 29, 30, 32, 33, 35, 37, 38, 60, 61, 65, 67, 68, 69, 71, 72, 73
demographic characteristics, 2, 3, 6, 7, 8, 9, 17, 38, 46, 80
Department of Justice, 1, 23, 27, 34, 35, 38, 73, 74

distribution, 47, 54, 85
District of Columbia, 10, 12, 13, 15, 23, 24, 30, 37

E

enforcement, vii, 2, 5, 18, 21, 22, 27, 28, 29, 31, 32, 33, 35, 36, 37, 39, 45, 47, 49, 50, 51, 54, 55, 59, 61, 65, 66, 68, 69, 70, 71, 72
ethnicity, 17

F

Federal Bureau of Investigation (FBI), 1, 4, 17, 22, 28, 31, 32, 34, 35, 37, 38, 39, 72
federal law, 21
felon, 34
financial, 23
funds, 34

G

Georgia, 11, 12, 14, 15, 24, 31, 63
Google, 28, 29, 71
governor, 24
grouping, 44
guidance, 71

H

Hawaii, 10, 12, 14, 15, 61, 64
health, 17, 18, 66, 67
Hispanic population, 55, 85
homicide, 1, 2, 4, 5, 28, 36, 37, 38, 39, 44, 45, 47, 49, 51, 54, 58, 59, 60, 68, 72, 85
homogeneity, 79
human, 39
hypothesis, 83

I

identification, 36, 65, 70, 71
improvements, 33, 36, 71
incidence, 34
independence, 31
Indians, 6, 7, 8, 9, 17
individuals, 21
inferences, 38, 39
injury, 1, 5, 6, 27
intoxication, 1, 3, 4, 27
Iowa, 10, 11, 13, 15, 61, 62
issues, 49

J

jurisdiction, 9, 10, 11, 12, 13, 14, 16, 19, 20, 24, 38, 71

L

law enforcement, vii, 1, 2, 3, 4, 5, 6, 18, 19, 20, 21, 22, 27, 28, 29, 30, 31, 32, 33, 34, 35, 36, 37, 38, 44, 45, 46, 47, 48, 49, 50, 51, 52, 53, 54, 55, 56, 57, 58, 59, 60, 61, 62, 65, 66, 67, 68, 69, 70, 71, 72, 76, 85
lead, 24
legislation, 21, 23, 70
Louisiana, 10, 12, 13, 15, 24, 63

M

magnitude, 47, 49
majority, 55, 65, 67
management, 23
Maryland, 11, 12, 14, 15, 24, 31, 61, 63
measurement, 55, 73
media, 22, 23, 38, 61, 65, 70, 72
medical, 21, 22, 23, 35, 37, 61, 65, 66, 70, 71
mental health, 21
methodology, 22, 27, 28, 29, 30, 32, 34, 36, 37, 38, 48, 60, 61, 65, 70, 71

Mexico, 11, 12, 14, 15, 25, 64
Missouri, 10, 11, 13, 15, 61, 62
models, 34, 74
modifications, 44
Montana, 10, 12, 14, 15, 24, 31, 61, 64

N

NIBRS, 72
NSA, 21

O

Office of Justice Programs, 73, 74
officials, 24
Oklahoma, 10, 12, 13, 15, 25, 63
online media, 24
overlap, 31, 42, 44, 50, 54, 61, 73, 79

P

Pacific Islanders, 7, 8, 9, 17
pairing, 41, 43
pilot study, 29
police, 16, 18, 19, 20, 22, 23, 24, 34, 39, 71, 73
population, 1, 31, 36, 39, 40, 44, 45, 46, 47, 48, 49, 59, 76, 79, 80, 81, 82, 85
primary data, 60, 71
prisons, 23, 29, 37
probability, 38, 41, 42, 43, 44, 46, 49, 54, 55, 73, 75, 80, 86
program staff, 61
public safety, 23, 66

R

race, 17, 40, 41, 47, 48, 54, 55, 56, 57, 58, 69, 74, 75, 80, 82, 83, 85
random numbers, 44
rape, 17, 18
recommendations, iv, 73
reliability, 71, 72
replication, 40, 42, 46, 51
requirement(s), 23, 29, 33, 39, 48, 55, 71, 82
researchers, 21
resources, 31, 37
response, 29, 37, 46, 71

S

SAS, 86
scaling, 43
scope, 21, 30, 36, 37, 38, 44, 72
search terms, 72
sensitivity, 55
sex, 40, 41, 42, 44, 49, 51, 69, 74, 77, 78, 79, 80
Social Security, 39
software, 86
South Dakota, 10, 11, 13, 15, 62
stakeholders, 71
state(s), vii, 1, 4, 5, 6, 11, 12, 22, 23, 24, 27, 28, 29, 30, 35, 36, 37, 38, 39, 55, 60, 61, 62, 63, 64, 65, 66, 69, 70, 71, 72, 85
statistics, vii, 34, 66, 67
suicide, 27, 39

T

tactics, 29
techniques, 39, 45
theft, 17, 18
theoretical assumptions, 48
transformation, 74
transport, 17, 18

U

United States, 1, 17, 28, 30, 31, 32, 35, 36, 37, 49, 50, 59, 69, 70, 71, 73
universe, 32, 35, 37, 50, 51, 60, 70, 71, 72

V

variables, 40, 41, 42, 44, 46, 48, 55, 73, 74, 75, 79, 82
variations, 70
victims, 54, 55, 58

W

Washington, 11, 12, 14, 15, 64, 73, 74
weapons, 24, 29
web, 29, 34, 72
websites, 24, 71, 72
Wisconsin, 10, 11, 13, 15, 25, 31, 63

Y

yield, 47, 82